Tales from the Big House: Normanby Hall

Tales from the Big House: Normanby Hall

400 years of its history and people

Stephen Wade

PEN & SWORD HISTORY

First published in Great Britain in 2017 by
Pen & Sword HISTORY
an imprint of
Pen & Sword Books Ltd
47 Church Street
Barnsley
South Yorkshire
S70 2AS

ISBN 978 1 47389 339 9

Typeset in Ehrhardt by
Mac Style Ltd, Bridlington, East Yorkshire

Printed and bound in Malta
By Gutenberg Press Ltd.

Pen & Sword Books Ltd incorporates the Imprints of
Pen & Sword Archaeology, Atlas, Aviation, Battleground, Discovery,
Family History, History, Maritime, Military, Naval, Politics, Railways,
Select, Transport, True Crime, Fiction,
Frontline Books, Leo Cooper, Praetorian Press,
Seaforth Publishing, Wharncliffe and White Owl.

For a complete list of Pen & Sword titles please contact
PEN & SWORD BOOKS LIMITED
47 Church Street, Barnsley, South Yorkshire, S70 2AS, England
E-mail: enquiries@pen-and-sword.co.uk
Website: www.pen-and-sword.co.uk

Contents

Introduction

You think that the contours of the place are familiar: the noble pile as seen on a thousand television programmes; the backdrop for the world of *Brideshead Revisited* and *Gosford Park*; you think that, for one moment as you look at the frieze on the wall and the peacocks calling from the yard, this is some unreal dream about a time when life seemed simpler, when everyone knew their place and every day was circumscribed and repeated. Ghosts are obligatory: there is surely a Grey Lady walking the corridors? You expect to hear the tinkling of champagne glasses and desultory talk of hunts and shoots; there is a sense that these walls have retained the voices, the emotions and the aspirations of those stylish and wealthy people of past times.

But no, a contemporary voice snaps you out of the reverie. Someone asks for money or for a season payment card. You are entering that very English creation, the country house as a business enterprise, as a quintessential aristocratic experience. Yet in spite of the cold light of reason as a closer and more sober inspection follows, that nagging, insistent feeling that history is here preserved more strongly than in any other dwelling tends to persist. The overall impression is that in places such as this, power was part of the lifestyle, and it was combined with *panache*.

That was the sensation I experienced the first time I visited Normanby Hall in North Lincolnshire after its new life in the hands of the local council. Even the word 'council' seemed wrong. Surely, I reflected, there was a squire inside, enjoying a G&T, perusing *Country Life* magazine? There must be a man in a smart outfit to polish the silver?

No, there was none of this. In fact, the absence of all this, and the sense that the reverie was ended, made me more determined than ever to tell the story of the Hall and to pluck from history the 'people stories' that are not usually found in the glossy guidebooks. The last thing I wanted to write was such a publication; my aim was a social history, with biographies interwoven. The work for that was a delight, full of discoveries, and never was the feeling that history is written by the powerful more persistent; therefore, all the more determined was my aim of including ordinary folk. But at the same time, the various family members of the Sheffield dynasty have offered fascinating stories too.

Recounting the history of a country house is inevitably to gather a bundle of tales, all concerned with the house's place and influence. Every such home across the acres of England has been a hub of employment, culture and economic importance, and Normanby is no exception. At first I envisaged the story of a family, but I ended with an account of, metaphorically, a spider in the centre of a constantly spun web. How could anyone have lived in the North Lincolnshire villages of Normanby, Winterton, Flixborough or the places that were to form Scunthorpe, through the centuries, and not be influenced by the remarkable Sheffield family? They must have featured in the breakfast talk of thousands of workers and their families, and their doings were surely reported on in local newspapers every week.

Consequently, I came to realize that I was dealing with an example of a solid, inescapable presence in the history of our land. One could almost use the word 'iconic' because the very mention of the phrase 'country house' has a resonance in the mind, as well as presenting an image.

As the visitor walks through the gates of Normanby Hall today, it takes an effort of historical imagination to see what the view would have been around 1830, when the Hall was new and had only the few essential outbuildings that were needed at that time. Today, that view from the little road to Normanby village includes a car park and kiosk, a gift shop, a fenced road out and a clutter of smaller structures, down to the information hut. If one removes all the later spread of heritage support installation, what is left is very much what the Regency place would have been, with Hall and stables dominating. Sir Robert Sheffield at that time would have looked out from his library to the left of the entrance hall to see grass and trees, and from his dining room on the other side he would have seen the parkland and beyond that, the territory of the hunter and stalker, nudging next to farming land.

It is not so hard today to imagine that Regency scene. Fortunately we have plenty of pictures and descriptions to help. Yet there is much more to a 'big house' than the mere verbal descriptions. Normanby, like all its kindred homes across England's verdant land, is a visible image of a way of life that has been part of the scene since the first lords of the manors after 1066, when William the Conqueror allotted land to his friends and fighters. The great Domesday Book, prepared from 1066 to 1086, is the first concept of that nation parcelled out to the victors, the beginnings of the Norman and Saxon oppositions that would eventually settle into a full and governed state, with a parliament and a set of laws. Survival is about stability, and in the case of English history, the seats of local power and status gradually evened out to become the centres of administration with the responsibility that went with it. The lords often became justices and Lords Lieutenants of shires or sheriffs, and so the country house became important for many, layered reasons.

When we walk to those gates today at Normanby, the end of that great chain of history is still there to see, albeit without its resident lords and servants. In past times, publications noted the problems inherent in writing about the Hall. In *Country Life*, for instance, in a feature from 1911, the author comments, 'In the Case of Normanby Park ... the difficulty of tracing the story is the greater, because the records in possession of the Sheffield family are remarkably scant.' This is not really the case for the modern period, but the earlier, pre-Tudor people and events are rather sketchy.

Received wisdom tells us that we generally fail to truly understand that which is on our doorstep; visitors to tourist locations are often amazed at the lack of knowledge exhibited by locals about the history and narratives concerning the place in question. I feel this to be true in my own case with regard to Normanby Hall, which sits in the rural heart of North Lincolnshire just a few miles from the steel town of Scunthorpe, where I have lived for forty years. I am a Yorkshireman, and by now I should be a Lincolnshire 'Yellowbelly', but that has never been the case. Strangely, after all these years of life just a few miles from the blast furnaces and rolling mills, part of me still feels like a visitor.

That strange and very English aspect of place and belonging is strikingly interesting with regard to our attitudes to country houses. We pay money to visit them and we stroll around the luscious libraries, dining rooms and halls with a sense of awe. This opulence and impressively beautiful feast for our eyes is something that is close to our homes, part of the scene, and yet oddly alien. The life of the seated family in their grand house is still almost mythically English; the success of *Downton Abbey* on television proves this. The immense popularity of this drama, featuring the lives of Lord Grantham and his family and their servants, has shown conclusively that our fascination with the aristocracy and their homes knows no bounds.

It is not simply the buildings and rooms that fascinate either: the *objets d'art*, paintings, furniture and lines of leather-bound volumes also intrigue us. The material culture of the rich and famous also draws us in. When Normanby Hall became leased to Scunthorpe Borough Council in 1964, a sale of house contents was needed, and entries from that catalogue tell us immediately what kinds of attractions lay within these great and stately places: 'A beautiful garniture of three Dresden vases as baskets of open latticework tinted in puce and turquoise and painted with naturalistic banquets' or 'An elegant William IV naval dress sword ... a Turkish sword ...' The catalogue listed such items as fenders, chandeliers, chests, vases, cupboards, wardrobes, cabinets, elbow chairs and window frames.

As Scunthorpe generally was primarily interested in the new stand for the football ground at the Old Show Ground or the fact that a garage man in Manley Street was cutting two pence off petrol, life in the early 1960s was dour and workmanlike for most. But 6 miles up the road, by Normanby village, there was a house and a park that symbolized another kind of Englishness: something rooted in traditional rural life. When it closed as a true family home in 1964, it was a very emotional occasion. What it represented was elegance, class and luxury, but also something else: its family story – its tales concerning people as well as buildings. That family story has its oddness and eccentricity. Those features have always been a part of high-class biography, as in the case of Sir William Ponsonby Barker, who used a female servant in place of a hot water bottle at his home at Cilcooley Abbey. But the family stories also exemplified the English family in general, somehow strangely exaggerated and more visible.

What the rich families did with their time also has its fascination. Roger Lewis, reviewing a new book on country homes, offers some figures that illustrate what many aristocrats did to fill the leisure hours: 'During the day the men went shooting. In the 1934–35 season, the Duke of Portland killed

5,148 pheasants and 3,268 brace of partridge at Welbeck Abbey. He was reticent compared with George V, however, who, with his group, slaughtered 3,937 pheasants … near Beaconsfield in a single day in 1913.'

Yet for much of the time, the owners and estate managers did work very hard and worried a great deal, having the huge responsibility of keeping the business going, for that was what the stately homes were, and are: businesses as well as leisure attractions. The Sheffield family in the nineteenth and early twentieth centuries, led by first Sir Robert and then by Sir Berkeley, have ample evidence in their records and archives proving that preserving such an estate is a constant worry. The life of Sir Robert illustrates this in every way, as the chapter on him shows. He produced an immense amount of written material, all concerned with practical estate management and farming topics. Sir Berkeley, his son, found time to be a Member of Parliament and to work for a time as a diplomat with Lord Milner.

Normanby Hall has been a perfect example of that phenomenon, the country home and estate that digs itself deeply into the locality and earns respect and affection. The Hall itself has changed and been adapted over the years, just as its families have had to change and adapt. But at the very heart of the enterprise there has always been the knowledge in the environs that it is a visible proof of something quintessentially English. It has reached out into fetes, processions, rural shows, miniature railways and even into hospital work, but here it has always stood, grand and immovable. Perhaps the closest instance we have in which the Hall was almost destroyed is during the Second World War when an unexploded bomb landed very close and was entrenched in the garden. But somehow it seems typical of the place that it survived and the bomb lay silently threatening, but inert.

Evidence of the Sheffield family's impact on the area around Burton, Normanby and Scunthorpe is not hard to find. The local press has chronicled their activities, and right up to its most recent newsworthy phase when Samantha Cameron (Samantha Sheffield at birth) married David Cameron, there has always been something of interest going on at 'the Hall'. If we take a distant view and look at Normanby from the air or from a train, then the image is a strikingly arresting one. This is because from the edge of the Park where eventing and dog walking go on regularly, there is a clear view of the steelworks that lies between Appleby and Scawby. Until the 1980s, there was also the massive plant of Normanby Park steelworks, though that has gone and has been replaced by a scattering of small companies strung out along the road between Scunthorpe and Burton.

As with all social history, a focus on one community brings the inevitable dual narrative of a micro and a macro history. The micro history tells the story of the Hall and the Park and how these played an important role in the development of the immediate rural area; it was a case of tenant farmers and close liaison between Hall and the dependent families, of course, and there is no denying that the knowledge behind the profit motive of the landowner is clearly in evidence in the archives; there was no room for any soft, indulgent attitudes when survival was the aim. In the macro history the story of the Hall reaches into world affairs at times, and certainly into the broader economic history of the countryside. Through the nineteenth century, there were rhythmic movements of boom and depression in agriculture and in keeping animals, and there were also periods when crime came to the fore, as with the always present threat of poaching on the large estates, and Normanby was no exception. The criminal element figures in the account of Sir Robert Sheffield in particular, as there were killings on his property as keepers and poachers clashed.

If one selects the real spine of the Sheffield family story since about 1800, it lies in the lives of the heads of the family at a time when the super rich were multiplying. The industrial revolution of the nineteenth century meant that the *nouveaux riches*, the wealthy men who had made their fortunes through business enterprise, were rubbing shoulders with the likes of the Sheffields, Portlands and Lowthers. From the Regency years through to the death of Queen Victoria, there was a certain sense of competition and of 'keeping up' with the need to have visible signs of status and wealth, and Normanby Hall did, to a limited extent, suffer from the results of that, but there is no doubt that at the point when it became pretty much what it is to the visitor today, it was developed in line with the current classical trends, as the great architect Robert Smirke set about making it notably impressive. Columns and porticos were the order of the day, and as Mordaunt Crook, architectural historian, has explained, classical structure and embellishment was hard to resist: 'The lure of classicism never had much to do with comfort or convenience. Ever since Alexander Pope, the Palladian mansion had been a byword for haughty discomfort: "Is this a dinner? This a genial room? / No, 'tis a temple and a hecatomb.'" It would have been understandable if Sir Robert Sheffield had gone along with such trends, but he and Smirke knew that classical design still had to be an image with a real, genuine domestic place behind the frontages. Mordaunt Crook sums up the appeal of Smirke: 'His austere neo-Classicism struck just the right note of dignity and restraint.'

The result, still very much in evidence today, is a fine, solid and appealing house: even a brief inspection leads one to conclude that this is a place that has been lived in. The visitor today will see, in spite of the fact that it has had to yield to the demands of the heritage industry and hold exhibitions and displays, there is still on view a nursery, a dining room and a library, and they look very much like rooms that knew family life. Perhaps the most telling detail of this sense of a lived-in stately home is the survival of the pet cemetery out in the grounds, where beloved animals were interred in years gone by.

My history, then, is far more than a guide for browsing callers in search of a commentary on the exhibits; the following chapters tell the wider story of the Sheffields and their workers, friends, tenants and guests. It is a social history with biographies integrated into the chapters. Some of the people and events may be simply tiny footnotes to history, but others were clearly playing a part in major events on the world stage. One of my aims is to show that Normanby Hall was never any kind of odd anachronism; on the contrary, it was at the hub of communal life over the centuries, but the narrative begins with an account of the Sheffield family and their origins. The history of Normanby Hall is really a group biography spanning centuries, but it is helpful to begin with the owners and their lives as they touched on great events.

Much of the commentary on landed estates and wealthy aristocrats in Victorian literature was critical, and a common attitude was perhaps encapsulated in a character called Mr Longestaff, in Anthony Trollope's novel *The Way we Live Now* (1875), of whom we have this description:

He was immensely proud of his position in life, thinking himself to be immensely superior to all those who earned their bread. There were, no doubt, gentlemen of different degrees, but the English gentleman of gentlemen was he who had land, and family title deeds and an old family place and family portraits ... and family absence of any usual employment.

Yet, in truth, this is not an accurate picture of any of the Sheffield baronets in the modern period. They might have had the land and the portraits, but they were profoundly involved in the work all around them.

I approached the preparatory work for the book with a spirit of someone entering familiar ground: that is, I expected stereotypes and figures from social comedy even. What I found was an organic community, with every person linked to others in the hierarchy. Of all the elements of English life through the centuries, since we first had the demesnes apportioned by William the Conqueror after 1066, the manor and its dependent community stands as an integral and unmoveable part of life. Of course, the lords with land and estates have all but gone, surviving in individual cases such as Prince Charles's domain, but there is something alluring about the old 'master' or 'squire' of English art and literature; the Sheffield baronets fit that perfectly. Looking back at the first Sir Robert's time, beginning in the later Regency, for instance, the modern reader sees someone who looks steadily at every square yard of his land, has one eye always on profit margins, and wants dedication and efficiency all around the estate.

But Sir Robert also cared. That comes across in what he left, and I had the sense, during all my digging up of the past, that the Sheffields and their Normanby land always had something tugging at their coat tails, like a needy child – it was the sense that they were looking after the home and the land; it was their turn to be caretakers, and to be aware of what was being handed on.

Chapter 1

The Family and the Place

One strong man in a blatant land.
Whatever they call him, what care I
Aristocrat, democrat, autocrat – one
Who can rule and dare not lie …

Mariana, by Alfred, Lord Tennyson

In looking at an English story, with its crowds of people, all reaching out to varied lives from the very centre of their hearth and home, the character of the place in which they grew up and learned about life is the basis of those intricacies of social history that inevitably follow. The Sheffield family is no exception, and in this case, the location of their home is Normanby Hall, a place very close to Burton-upon-Stather on the Humber's banks, and to a cluster of North Lincolnshire villages to the south. A little beyond that is the town of Scunthorpe, whose 'four Queens' – blast furnaces of the steelworks – always seem to take centre stage on the horizon.

In the 1920s, W.F. Rawnsley gave this very comprehensive description of this area, starting with Burton:

In the village is a really beautiful old Tudor house of brick, with stone mullions, called Walcot Old Hall, the property of J. Goulton Constable. The little isolated bit of chalk wold which begins near Walcot is but 4 miles long, and in the centre of it is perched the village of Burton-upon-Stather. The church stands on the very edge of the cliff, and a steep road leads down to the staithe, a ferry landing stage … here we stopped to admire the delightful view.

The Trent was just below us … across the Trent lay the Isle of Axholme, green but featureless, and beyond it the sinuous Ouse. … We leave the village by an avenue of overarching trees and cross the wold obliquely, passing Normanby Hall, the residence of Sir B.D. Sheffield, many of whose ancestors lie buried in Burton Stather Church.

Family history at its most basic level is still a considerable challenge for the historian and researcher. There is always a mix of occupations and events involved, and the challenge for the reader is to make sense of the interrelationships, and of course to look for stories that tend to move laterally, alongside the bare outline and lists of names. This was first apparent with reference to the Sheffield family of Normanby when I came across a scribbled attempt to provide a tree, and this showed that between John Sheffield's eventful life in the seventeenth century through to the death of Sir Berkeley Sheffield in 1946, there was so much material in such a small space that facts crowded out any clear line of ascent through the years.

The Hall in its first inception belonged to the Hildyard family of Winestead, and it was bought in 1510 from Sir Christopher Hildyard by Nicholas Girlington. Then, in 1589, it was sold to Lord Edmund Sheffield, who became the first Earl of Mulgrave, and died in 1646. His grandson built the Restoration house, following from a Tudor building, and that grandson was the first Duke of Buckingham and Normanby: John Sheffield.

I shall resume the story of the Sheffield baronetcy shortly, but first a brief diversion into earlier history is needed, when the Sheffield men were warriors, players in power games and above all, people standing together in times when kin meant strength when there was no dependable law machine and you could not ring for the police when in trouble.

The Sheffields go back in time well before John Sheffield, the famous figure of Stuart history. In fact, as Sir Reginald Sheffield has explained, the Sheffield origins are in a certain Sir Robert at the time of the Crusades. This noble knight's tomb is in St Andrew's Church at Burton-upon-Stather. He was in fact a Templar, and this order later became, in the words of Sir Reginald, 'a kind of aristocratic "Foreign Legion" including among their members not only seekers after God and heroism but also increasing numbers of failures, disappointed lovers, restless ambitious men ...' All that is known about this first Sheffield is that he took part in the Fifth Crusade, and he was followed by a string of other Sheffields, down to a William Sheffield, who was Dean of York at the time when the Battle of Bosworth Field brought the end of the Yorkists and the beginnings of the Tudor dynasty when Richard III was killed.

At that point the Sheffields moved into the Isle of Axholme and West Butterwick. In the Middle Ages through to the Tudor years, the family were engaged in the essential business of making beneficial marriages in order to strengthen their position and to ensure future success. They really began to come into prominence in the reign of Henry VIII when a Sir Robert was Speaker of the House of Commons. Sir Reginald's account says something more about this particular Sir Robert: 'He built a great fortified brick tower at West Butterwick on the lines of Tattershall Castle and also had a fine house in Hammersmith.' He was painted by the great Hans Holbein, and that is surely a mark of his power and status.

The Sheffields were later involved in national events, such as the rebellion of John Kett, and a John Sheffield took on the rebels, in charge of a mercenary force. It is plain to see that the Sheffields, up to the early seventeenth century, were skilful at cultivating the arts of survival, making alliances and forming friendships to retain fundamental advantages. Typical of their status and influence is the fact that at the time of the Spanish Armada in 1588, Edmund Sheffield was in the ranks of the council of war, and later he was made a Knight of the Garter; by 1609, he was Lord President of the North, which, as Sir Reginald explains, meant that 'he governed the whole of the North of England.' He was a man of action and an entrepreneur on the largest scale, even being involved in financing colonization in the new 'Americas'. The writer of the *Country Life* feature, mentioned in my introduction, provides startling information on this adventurer and man of action: 'In James I's reign he tried to quiet the suspicions raised by his marriage with a Roman Catholic by harrying the Papists very zealously. ... At the coronation of Charles I he received his earldom but he turned against the king. ... Of his twenty children, one daughter must be mentioned because she became the mother of Black Tom, the great Lord Fairfax.' It has to be said that Edmund and his family are surely prime candidates for fictional treatment.

Edmund's portrait lies in the National Maritime Museum at Greenwich, and there he sits, with a swagger, one arm akimbo and a facial expression that hints at his toughness. He had a long life (1565–1646) and was always involved in some kind of business and opposition; in the Armada conflict he commanded no less than three ships, perhaps most prominently, *The White Bear*. It was in 1591 that he was given the property of Mulgrave in Yorkshire and he became Lord Lieutenant of the shire.

This Sheffield and his son figure in fiction also; in fact, in the classic North Lincolnshire novel of the seventeenth century, *The MS in a Red Box* by John Hamilton. There is an intriguing story behind this book: in 1903, the manuscript arrived at the publisher Bodley Head in London, but there was no name nor any address attached. The publisher liked it and wanted to publish it, and so they advertised to try to attract the attention of the author, but to no avail. It was then published in 1904. Today, after research, it is almost certain that it was written by a congregational minister at Crowle – a man who would have known the Sheffield lands when they, as the Earls of Mulgrave, owned much of Axholme.

But Hamilton makes the Sheffields the villains in the novel, which concerns the strife between the Axholme men who want the land to be left alone, and the followers of the Dutch engineer Cornelius Vermuyden, and Sheffield, who want it reclaimed and developed in such a way that old patterns of life and work would go on. This passage shows how the Sheffields are textualized:

> My mind was filled with apprehension, which I could not express. That Sheffield could do an act of pure kindness was incredible. His foul pursuit of beauty was a byword in the Isle, and there were fathers, brothers and lovers who were held back from murderous revenge only by terror of the old Earl, who had long been President of the Council of the North, and consequently held unlimited authority over the common people of Axholme. Even that fear might not have restrained some, but Sheffield … always went armed and attended, and had a host of spies in his pay.

This depiction of the Earl does not appear to be founded on any evidence, but it makes for a good, dramatic story.

Resuming the story of the Sheffield earls, dukes and baronets, it helps to begin with a list, so reference may be made to this when names may become confusing, especially when there is more than one person with the same forename. Here they are, in chronological order:

Lord Edmund Sheffield (1st Earl Mulgrave): died 1646

Edmund Sheffield (2nd Earl Musgrave, son): died 1658

John Sheffield (1st Duke of Buckingham and Normanby): died 1721

Edmund Sheffield (son): died 1735

Charles Sheffield (half brother): died 1774, First Baronet

Sir John Sheffield: died 12 February 1815, Second Baronet

Rev Sir Robert Sheffield: died 26 February 1815, Third Baronet

Sir Robert Sheffield: died 1862, Fourth Baronet

Sir Robert Sheffield: died 1886, Fifth Baronet

Sir Berkeley Sheffield: died 1946, Sixth Baronet

Sir Robert Sheffield: died 1977, Seventh Baronet

(current) Sir Reginald Sheffield , born 1946

Before embarking on an outline of the baronets and the social context, it is useful to have a summary of the baronetcy from the point at which it became '*of Buckingham and Normanby*'. That is, from Sir Charles Sheffield, who was born in 1706, through to the death of Sir Berkeley Sheffield in 1946, as this book ends at that point. The reader might want to use this, and refer to it, as a point of reference, as such a genealogy may be very confusing.

1st Baronet:

People

Sir Charles Sheffield, born 1706 and married Margaret Sabine in April 1741; died 1774.

    Children: Sir John, Charles, Sir Robert, Anne, Alicia and Sophia. This is the man who sold Buckingham House, in St James' Park, to King George III for the sum of £21,000 – probably about £1.5 million in today's values.

Times and events

Sir Charles was made a baronet in 1755 – 'of Normanby in the county of Lincoln'. The early eighteenth century brought massive social changes, and Sir Charles had a long life, in which, as an estate owner, he would have felt the effects of such episodes as the social disorder that was recurrent through this time. The 1715 Riot Act was passed after serious rioting, and in the following years, it was the fear of offences against those who had property that impinged on the landowners' lives. For instance, The Black Act of 1723 was passed after an escalation of violence in poaching offences, and this was part of a string of legislation known as the 'Bloody code', which included a large number of capital offences for crime against property.

Also in Charles's time there was the Militia Act of 1757; this was passed in a climate of fear after a European war and the fear of possible invasion. The Act created a force of 60,000 men, and a man had to serve for three years. But Sir Charles was wealthy and so he and his family could avoid service because they could pay a fine or buy a substitute.

2nd Baronet:

People
Sir John Sheffield, born around 1743, and married Charlotte Digby in December, 1784. He died in February, 1815.

Times and events
Sir John's time included the desperate years of war with revolutionary France and then with Napoleon. He died early in the year that was to see Napoleon defeated at Waterloo. But in the last years of the eighteenth century, there was paranoia in the ranks of the rich and those in power, as there was a fear of the revolutionary spirit reaching Britain.

There were many statutes made in the 1790s that were to suppress individual or group radicalism. In 1792, for instance, there were proclamations against sedition, and in 1795, the 'Two Acts' of Treasonable and Seditious Practices made the law of treason applicable to spoken and written words.

3rd Baronet:

People
Rev Sir Robert Sheffield, born 1758, died 4 February 1815. First wife, Penelope Pitches, and second wife, Sarah Kennet. He had two children by his first wife (Robert and Penelope) and seven children by his second wife: Rev Charles and six daughters. He was to be 3rd Baronet for merely three weeks before his son succeeded.

Times and events
His short time as baronet saw the continuance of repressive legislation.

4th Baronet:

People
Sir Robert Sheffield, born 25 February 1786; died 7 November 1862. He married Julia Newbolt in October 1818. They had eight children, and Robert, the eldest, succeeded. He was Sheriff of Lincolnshire from 1817–18, and was chairman of the Kirton Lindsey Quarter Sessions.

Times and events
Sir Robert's time as baronet involved his work as chairman of magistrates, so he knew from close quarters what effects social change was having on the rural poor, and consequently on crime. For instance, it was in these years that enclosure escalated, and this displaced a great number of people whose work had been on the common land. Enclosure made common land into fenced property, and so there was an increase in maximising production of food and the breeding and rearing of animals for meat. From 1760 to 1799 there were about 1,600 Enclosure Acts. Also important for his work was the Justices Qualification Act of 1744, as this stipulated that the Justice had to have land with an annual value of £100.

He would have also lived through the time of Corn Law agitation. These laws started in 1815 and continued for thirty years, the aim being to increase food imports and reduce food exports. Obviously this would increase the pressure on the rural poor and cause industrial depressions. The laws were repealed in 1846.

His age was also the 'Railway Age', and by 1852, the railway network had extended considerably. By 1850, there was the Midland Railway and the 'East Coast route' from London to Edinburgh and Glasgow, and in the year of his death, the Great Eastern Railway was created after some amalgamations. His land was not so far from Doncaster, which by 1854 was the locomotive headquarters for the Great Northern Railway.

On the bench passing sentences to local criminals, Sir Robert would come to know the reasons behind such offences as petty theft, poaching and other regular small offences, but he also had to deal with serious crime such as assault, rape and even murder. Transportation to Tasmania stopped in the 1850s and the year before his death, the Offences Against the Person Act was passed, revising the whole of the criminal law in that context.

In agriculture generally, his years in the seat of power saw technology really start to have an impact. For instance, as T.W. Beastall notes in his agricultural history of the county, 'Anthony Hammond reported on the implements to be seen at Lincoln in 1854 where machinery worth £28,878 was on show from 130 exhibitors submitting 1,897 articles.'

5th Baronet:

People
Sir Robert Sheffield, born 8 December 1823; died 23 October 1886. The second Sir Robert was running the Hall and Park from 1862 to the time of his death in 1886. He married Priscilla Dumaresq in 1867 and they had four children. His daughter Gwendoline married the very rich Lancelot Lowther, the Earl of Lonsdale; his daughter Helen married the equally rich and powerful Hugh, 1st Duke of Westminster, and his other daughter, Dorothy, married into yet another wealthy family, wedding the 7th Viscount Portman.

Times and events
This Sir Robert was an army man. He joined the Horse Guards ('the Blues') in 1842 and was a captain seven years later. His wife Priscilla was also from a military background, her father being a distinguished officer. At this time (c. 1840s–50s) there was plenty for the army to do, and the culmination of various diplomatic struggles was the Crimean War of 1853–56.

6th Baronet:

People
Sir Berkeley Sheffield, born 19 January 1876; died 26 November 1946. He married Baroness Julia van Tuyll in 1904, and they had four children.

Times and events
Sir Berkeley's assumption of the baronetcy in 1886 occurred at the time when modernity was just reaching into most areas of life. In agriculture there had been a sign of times to come with the establishment of the first agricultural workers' trade union in 1872. Technology had also arrived: there

had been reaping machines since 1851, but then came the establishment of such organizations as the Cattle Breeders' Association in 1907, and in the Sheffield's own county, there was the Lincolnshire Farmers' Union, which soon became the National Farmers' Union, formed in 1908.

There were massive wars, of course. Sir Berkeley's tenure saw the Anglo-Boer Wars of 1899–1902; the Great War of 1914–18 and the Second World War of 1939–45). In those years, Normanby Hall, his home, was in use as a military hospital and as a base for soldiers in the months before the momentous D-Day landings of 1944.

We begin with John Sheffield, who was Edmund's son. Here was a major figure in the history of his time. When very young he enlisted in the fleet that was commanded by Prince Rupert of the Rhine, and he was to participate in both naval battles and cavalry confrontations through to the 1670s. His life reads like that of a romantic adventurer at times, such as his fondness for Princess Anne, which so upset her father, Charles II. How could he win back his good name?: by leading a force to take back the port of Tangiers, which had been lost to the Ottoman Empire, of course. It didn't work out well, but he survived, and when the new king, James II, came along, John was advanced still more, to the office of Privy Councillor. Later, when Protestantism was restored with William of Orange and Queen Mary, John remained in favour, and he became very rich; he was made Marquis of Normanby, and so the 'dynasty' began.

The end of John Sheffield's story is that, as he had been close to Anne, when she became Queen Anne, John was appointed President of the Council, and surely one of his finest actions was the establishment of Buckingham Palace in 1703. He spent the end of his life there, and by any standard, his achievements had been incredibly impressive. As historian Winston Kime has put it, 'He held office under four sovereigns. ... He gave unswerving loyalty to the Stuarts.'

But that is not all there was to this remarkable 1st Duke of Buckingham. He was also a poet and man of letters. He wrote essays and poems and was best known in his time for his 'Essay on Satire', which was passed around in manuscript, enjoyed for its poking fun at celebrities of what we would call today the 'glitterati'. John Sheffield lived until 1721, and in that year the bookseller and printer Edmund Curl (who was later to be a friend of Samuel

Johnson) published a pirated edition of Sheffield's poetry, and he was in serious trouble for breach of privilege, as explained below.

He was certainly of some status and esteem in literary affairs in the mid-eighteenth century, and the fact that his biography is included in Samuel Johnson's *Lives of the Poets*, published from 1779 to 1781, confirms that he had ability and was highly rated. Johnson wrote: 'His literary acquisitions are more wonderful, as those years in which they are commonly made were spent by him in the tumult of military life, or the gaiety of the court.' But when it came to the inclusion of a moral commentary on him, which Johnson always provided in his collection, there are criticisms, and these come as no surprise when we reflect on the sheer energy and enterprise in Sheffield's career. Johnson wrote:

> His character is not to be proposed as worthy of imitation. His religion he may be supposed to have learned from Hobbes, and his morality was such as naturally proceeds from loose opinions. His sentiments with respect to women he picked up in the court of Charles, and his principles concerning property were such as the gaming table supplies. He was censured as covetous and has been defended by an instance of inattention to his affairs, as if a man might not at once be corrupted by avarice and idleness. He is said, however, to have had much tenderness and to have been very ready to apologize for his violence of passion.

There is nothing exceptional or extreme in this censure; Johnson was always quick in his condemnation of biographical subjects, and he himself had episodes of extreme immorality. The fact is that, in Johnson's time, it was expected of a biographer that he would find the faults in a person. But at least we have the last sentence, which is a fine compliment.

Johnson, on the other hand, when he turns to Sheffield's writing, has good things to say at first, but then criticises harshly again. He notes that he was 'a poet of no vulgar rank' but goes on to write, 'His songs are upon common topics; he hopes and grieves and repents, and despairs, and rejoices, like any other maker of little stanzas; to be great he hardly tries; to be gay is hardly in his power.'

John Sheffield played a part in the life and writing of the great poet
Alexander Pope as well. George Sherburn, one of Pope's biographers in the
early twentieth century, recounted the saga of Pope's editing of Sheffield's
poems in an edition that was printed shortly after Sheffield's death. Their
relationship was well established by that time. When Pope wrote his great
poem *An Essay on Criticism*, he praised Sheffield, and in return, when in
1717 Pope's collected poems came out, Sheffield wrote in praise of Pope's
translation of *The Iliad*:

> *And yet so wondrous, so sublime a thing*
> *As the great Iliad, scarce could make me sing,*
> *Unless I justly could at once commend*
> *A good companion, and as firm a friend.*
> *One moral, or a mere well-natured deed*
> *Can all desert in sciences exceed*

Then, the publication of Sheffield's works caused a stir in Parliament when
the publisher Edmund Curll advertised that he was to publish 'the works of
the Right Honourable John Sheffield, Duke of Buckingham, in prose and
verse with his life … and a true copy of his last will and testament'. This
brought Curll into the House to answer a charge of Breach of the Privilege
of the House. This happened because the House of Lords had commanded
that after Sheffield's death, 'no person was to presume to publish his works
… without the consent of his heirs or executors.'

Curll retracted, and later Pope himself took over, and was editor of the
works. All the fuss about this was that some of Sheffield's poems could be
read as 'Jacobitical and seditious'. When Pope's edition came into print, as
the biographer Sherburn wrote, 'Then fell the thunderbolt! On Sunday,
27th 1721, the copies were seized by his Majesty's Messengers.' Pope
worked hard to have the prohibition removed, and at last, by 1723, some
were printed. It seemed that drama and controversy followed John Sheffield
all his life, and even after his death.

John Sheffield is the subject of an impressive monument in the Lady
Chapel of Westminster Abbey; he lies there with his wife, Catherine, and
their four children. This was the work of Denis Plumiere, and the sculptors

were Laurent Delvaux and Peter Scheemakers. As the commentary on the Abbey website summarizes:

> The life-size figure of the Duke, dressed in Roman armour and holding a baton, reclines on a mattress, while a figure of his wife mourns. ... A figure of Time carries away medallion relief portraits of three of the children. ... Sophia (died 1706), John, Marquis of Normanby (died 1710) and Henrietta Maria (died December 1717). A medallion of Robert, Marquis of Normanby (born 1711, died February 1715) is at his feet.

Sir Reginald's account of his ancestor notes that, 'The Duke was not only interested in political power; he was an eminent poet and a rather bad playwright. He was the patron of John Dryden and William Wycherley, two of the most important literary figures of the time.'

He was followed at Normanby by Edmund and then Charles; the former died very young and the latter, though illegitimate, had been placed in the position of legal heir of John, and he was made a baronet in 1755. It was he who sold Buckingham Palace in 1762 to King George III. From the time of the next Sheffield, Sir John, the ruling aristocrats became much more involved in the estate in North Lincolnshire.

In the time of Charles's son, Sir John, the 2nd Baronet, there was a touch of scandal in the family. It happened in November 1800, and this report from *The Courier and Evening Gazette* tells the tale, which involved that common eighteenth-century outrage, the elopement. The report is from a law summary from the King's Bench:

> A motion was made for a rule for criminal information against James Legatt. His offence was having obtained a licence to marry by means of a false oath. He had sworn his wife was 22 years of age when in fact she was only 20. He was a person of low condition in life, a trade what was called a keelman, and resided in Yorkshire, on the banks of the Humber. His wife was a lady of rank, daughter of Major General Thomas Cox, and niece to Sir John Sheffield. She had been at the house of the latter in the year 1799, when the defendant followed her, and she

soon after eloped with him. They were pursued to Hull, where it was discovered they had married by a licence, obtained in consequence of the defendant's swearing the lady was of age.

The result was that the court granted a 'rule to show cause', which meant that the court desired the party with the grievance (Cox) to establish or prove the fact on which the case rested: the woman's age. The case depended on the criminal information – in other words, it was a first step towards prosecution, showing the intention of the plaintiff. Cox obviously demanded some punishment from the law. His daughter had been seduced and taken away, with an intention to deceive by telling an untruth at a divine service.

It seems incredible that a keelman should have arrived at the Hall and persuaded the woman to elope with him. But there is an affair of the heart here, overriding class hierarchy, of course. As to Legatt being a keelman, this meant that he worked on the keels or barges that loaded coal on to the collier ships. This was hard, seasonal work, usually with a one-year contract, and involved collecting coal from a riverside chute and then taking it to the ships on an ebb tide.

Abduction, if it could be proved, could at that time have been a capital offence. One case in Dublin ended in a hanging, as this criminal tale announced to the reader:

The case of Mr Dan Kimberley, attorney at law, executed at Dublin, 27 May 1730, for assisting Bradock Mead to marry Bridget Rending, an heiress. Contained in his declaration and dying words, delivered to the Rev Mr Derry, at the place of execution, and recommended to Dean Percival, John Hacket, Esq, and two other gentlemen, to see it published. Price: three pence.

But in Legatt's case, the likely outcome was a prison sentence or, given the date of the offence, a stretch serving in the army, as militias were being raised at the time, war with France being in progress.

We can only imagine the talk of scandal at the Hall as the eighteenth century ended with this tale of romantic love or deplorable seduction, whatever was the truth of the business.

In 1769, there occurred one of those sad morality tales that fill the pages of Georgian social history: the brother of the 3rd Baronet, Sir Robert (who died in 1815), was Charles Jacob Sheffield, and the family tree shows that he died without issue; at what date is uncertain. The reason for this is that he was destined to be a sad inhabitant of the debtor's prison in London: the Marshalsea.

Charles Jacob was an ensign in the Coldstream Guards, which is the lowest stage on the ladder of officer class. The ranks back then had to be bought in almost all cases, so he was, for reasons unknown, to have an army career and did not marry. In 1769, he fell into financial problems, owing the immense sum of £240 to a certain William Spencer of Clerkenwell. Charles, we know from an affidavit, was earning '£90 or thereabouts' per annum at the age of 21 in 1769, and he became legally bound to pay an annuity to Spencer as a way out of his problem.

That problem was that he had been imprisoned initially; it took until April 1770 for a court to arrange release and have a settlement made on Spencer. The ruling was that William Spencer was 'undefended against the said Charles' and so:

> it is considered that the said William recover against the said Charles his said debt and also sixty-three shillings for his damages which he has sustained as well by occasion of the detaining of that debt as for his costs and charges by him about his suit in that behalf ... awarded by the court of our said Lord the King now how adjudged to the said mercy – William by his agent and the said Charles in money.

In other words, Charles's family had worked to have him released on the understanding that the outstanding debt and the costs would be paid by annuity. There would be no chance of Charles losing the income before paying out.

How he acquired the debt is unknown. At that time, gambling was common in the aristocracy, and the debtors' prisons were full of apparently successful high status people. For instance, in a list of insolvent debtors compiled by Lindsey Withers, we have cordwainers, peruke-makers, husbandmen, brokers, grocers, millers, carvers, gilders and carpenters. But we also have

'Susanna Westcott, late of Brampford Speke in the county of Devon, widow'. In fact, there was always a steady flow of artists, writers and actors swelling the cells in the Marshalsea and the Fleet, where many debtors were held.

Debt was a common part of life, as it is now. In a cartoon of 1830 by Henry Heath, he shows a debtor being served with a writ, with the caption 'Too civil by half' as the pursuer almost faints with fatigue in pursuit of his prey. *The Gentleman's Magazine* in 1750 estimated that there were 20,000 debtors in jail. Usually, the imprisonment was just short term, but treatment could be cruel. Just thirty years before William was in jail, a committee of MPs looked at conditions for debtors, and found that there was 'barbarous and cruel treatment of debtor inmates in high violation and contempt of the laws of this kingdom'.

It was a fate suffered by many in the arts. There was humiliation and disgrace, of course; but we have a mass of information from artists and writers imprisoned for debt at that time and into the early Victorian years, and so we understand what William had to suffer. Benjamin Haydon, painter and friend of John Keats, painted scenes he saw in the King's Bench, and he kept a diary in which he wrote that he 'had to battle with creditors and get the next month as clear as possible to work.'

The gaols were limbos of neglect, with a range of punishments in the tough regimes maintained by the tyrants who held the keys and the food supplies. A few humanitarians occasionally tried to change things, but one additional problem was that offices and responsibilities of all kinds were up for sale, in an age of nepotism and corruption. The Georgian and Regency periods were times in which sinecures were bought and sold as a matter of everyday business. A publication called *The Red Book* listed these offices and their value. A typical example was the Wardenship of the Cinque Ports, which paid a thousand pounds a year. A celebrated case was that of Ashley Cowper, younger brother of William Cowper, who was a barrister in 1723. He was also a Mason and a member of the Horn Lodge. Ashley acquired the post of Clerk to the Parliaments, a very well paid and esteemed post. The post was in fact bought for him by his father, who just happened to be Judge Spence Cowper.

There was no investigation into nepotism and sinecures until 1780. The situation was, as historian Blake Pinnell has explained, that 'The law courts, the established church, part of the army and the Royal household contained many positions in which the occupants did very little for the money they received. Many of the people awarded the management of prisons never even saw the building, let alone inspected the prisons to check on conditions, and the debtors were sometimes mixing with felons.

In the management of prison, this was a very dangerous and destructive practice, particularly as the man who bought the governorship could stay away from the prison as often as he liked, and leave a minion in charge. One of the very worst of these abuses was highlighted in the case of John Huggins, warden of the Fleet prison, who was tried at the Old Bailey in 1729 for the murder of one of his charges, Edward Arne.

The only element that more than likely saved the life of Charles Jacob was that he could receive cash from outside, and therefore he could eat and drink, give 'garnish' (bribe) to the gaoler, and even walk outside the gaol for part of the day.

We are perhaps most familiar with the Marshalsea today because that was where Charles Dickens's father, John, was imprisoned for debt a generation after poor Charles Jacob Sheffield. The latter lived an eventful life, and in fact, three years after his release, we learn that he appeared at the Old Bailey, but this time as a victim, speaking at the trial of George Brown for violent theft and highway robbery. The Annual Register for 1774 reported that 'George Brown robbed Charles Jacob Sheffield on the highway near Knightsbridge of a gold watch and some money.'

In court, Charles stated: 'On 16 July, between ten and eleven in the evening, coming to town in a post-chaise, I was stopped at Knightsbridge by three foot-pads; they demanded my money and watch; I gave it to them; it was a gold watch.' He told the court that he never saw the watch again, 'John Fielding sent for me, and there I saw these (the seal and part of a chain). The other part of the chain was produced, which is the principal part that I can swear to, but the woman who had it is no more; her name is Elizabeth Grey; I can swear to the seal: I am sure it was to the watch.'

This is a momentous moment in the Sheffield family history. Here we have a family member who had all but disappeared from the annals of history, being released from prison, but perhaps financially crippled by paying out over a quarter of his earnings, but in fact he still uses a post chaise and has valuables. It appears that he is still in the army at this time, and incredibly, he refers to a beloved to whom he gave a chain. Another point is that he has met John Fielding, the brother of the novelist Henry Fielding, and the two brothers were at the time running Bow Street Court and dealing with thieves and receivers.

The Sheffield story has here touched on the mainstream of British criminal history, and but for the robbery, Charles Jacob would surely have disappeared into obscurity. Instead, we have his actual spoken words transcribed and written on the online text of the Old Bailey sessions records.

As Sir Reginald explains, it was Charles's grandson, Sir Robert, who became arguably the real driving force behind the identity of Normanby Hall and its land as the heart of the family and its progress: 'Charles's grandson, Sir Robert, finally sold his remaining properties in London and moved to live at Normanby. It is he who built the present house.' Sir Robert took over in the Regency period and he brought in the great architect Robert Smirke.

The home had been rebuilt by Edmund Sheffield at the end of the sixteenth century and the architect then was Robert Smythson (1535–1614), who also built such magnificent Tudor homes as Doddington Hall, near Lincoln, and Burton Agnes Hall, in East Yorkshire. The Tudor mansion had been the typical shaping of three turrets and three floors; the image was one of solidity mixed with more than a dash of elaborate presence and flair, with plenty of windows, as a show of wealth and 'modernity'. The Smythson concept was well described by Nikolaus Pevsner, the architectural historian:

They show a quadrangular plan of three storeys. What was built is known from a survey plan to have had distinct Smithson traits: excessive height and verticality, and the use of pergolas and balconies. Smithson was active in the East Midlands ... and quite abreast of the latest Elizabethan developments; well proportioned relation of window to wall, sparseness of elevation, and clean silhouette.

Typically for that style, the overall plan is an E shape, with pronounced length rather than depth. Other Smythson homes include Longleat House, Hardwick Hall and Wollaton Hall. Smythson's biography is obscure, but we know that he died at Wollaton in 1614 and on his memorial in the parish church there the inscription reads: 'Architecter [*sic*] and Surveyor unto the most worthy house of Wollaton and divers others of great account.' He started a dynasty of architects, as his son John and grandson Huntingdon followed in his trade. It is known that he started out as a stonemason and worked in London and Wiltshire.

Now in stepped Robert Smirke. This was a man who, born in 1780, was at the height of his career, creating architecture in the Greek revival style. He had a classical education and started his apprenticeship in architecture under Sir John Soane, though this had not worked out. Then, in 1796, he began studies at the Royal Academy and won a Silver Medal. He designed the British Museum in 1799 and then did what most wealthy young men did: he undertook the educational European Grand Tour. That experience inspired him to conceive of his aesthetics. He wrote:

How can I by description give you any idea of the great pleasure I enjoyed in the sight of these ancient buildings of Athens! How strongly were exemplified in them the grandeur and effect of simplicity in architecture!

The first great step forward for Smirke came in 1807 when he was contracted to design the Royal Mint. After that, he was always in demand, and his list of credits includes Lansdowne House, the British Museum and the General Post Office, along with the rebuilding of the Covent Garden Theatre. One rhyme written about him says a great deal about his status when he was employed at Normanby:

> *Go to work, rival Smirke*
> *Make a dash, a la Nash.*
> *Something try at, worthy Wyatt;*
> *Plans out carry, great as Barry.*

Pevsner, writing in 1960, was aware of later additions made by Walter Brierley (which will be discussed in Chapter 5), and he describes the Hall in precise technical ways:

The design typifies Smirke's 'cubic' style. It is an essay in intersecting cubes. The western front with slightly projecting two-storey wings, each with a tripartite window and a balustrade parapet. Between them a higher three-bay, three-storey centre with tapered windows to the upper floors and a porch of paired unfluted Ionic columns.

The design is fully appreciated if we imagine a set of cubes placed so as to create rooms with projected corners, so that each section of the building has the impression of several corners sticking out, making angular views.

Pevsner was particularly impressed by the attic and the chimney pieces, the latter being marble, and made by Richard Westmacott, the sculptor who produced the Achilles statue in Hyde Park and many other sculptures of famous figures in London and Birmingham.

Overall, the defining feature of the Hall is expressed in Smirke's dictum that 'Rectangular shapes are the component materials of every modern work.' If we need a simple example of this, then his assize court for Lincoln, inside the castle, shows this: the three rectangular sections, with the central one most prominent, and with the supporting rows of columns, shows this Gothic Revival trait at its most bold and typical.

Work started in the autumn of 1825, when the former Georgian hall was demolished, along with the old gatehouse. As well as the Hall itself there were the cottages and stables to build; the whole enterprise cost £29,161. It is difficult to estimate the cost giving a modern figure, but roughly, according to most sources for this, today's figure would be £12 million.

What about the locality? What was that like when the Hall appeared in its full glory in the 1820s? Local writers in the century before that date have given accounts of the place. At the end of the eighteenth century, for instance, the writer Abraham de la Pryme gave this opinion of Burton, the village on the Humber just a short walk from Normanby, and noted, 'I was at Burton and expected to have found a fine large town there, but I was much mistaken, it being but little and ill-built.' When he returned in 1697, the Hall was then in the hands of John Sheffield, and de la Pryme comments:

I went to Normanby. It is but a small hamlet belonging to Lord Mulgrave. ... He has a very fine well built hall or palace there but it is not great, nor very stately. From thence I went to Burton, which is a mile further. … The church is built of rough stone, and has nothing worth seeing in, there being no epitaphs, though there has been considerable men buried here, as the late Lord and Lady Mulgrave and others.

Francis Jarvis, writing in the early twentieth century, quotes an old manuscript that gives details of the years immediately before Sir Robert, the Fourth Baronet, took the reins in 1815, and we have there an account of the family in the years from 1774 to 1815, and this needs such an explanation because people died in a cluster before the new building was built and the regime of Sir Robert began:

Sir John [the second baronet] died in February 1815, and, leaving no issue, was succeeded in the Baronetcy and estates by his brother, the Reverend Sir Robert Sheffield; he was born on 1 December 1757, and in 1785 became rector of Flixborough and Vicar of Burton-upon-Stather. He married twice, his first wife being Penelope, daughter of Sir Abraham Pitches … by whom he had one son, Robert. … The Rev Robert Sheffield married secondly 3 December 1796, Sarah Anne, daughter of the Rev Brackly Kennett. … He succeeded to the baronetcy in February 1815, but survived his brother, Sir John Sheffield, Second Baronet, for only three weeks.

Consequently, Sir Robert, the Fourth Baronet, took over. Regarding the parkland, the same writer explains the environs, and his comments explain lots of practical reasons why the shaping of the local landscape was done; this was the template for future agriculture and for the wider context of all the family activities:

As was customary in former years, the Old Hall at Normanby was built in close proximity to the High Road … and from an existing map of the Park and surroundings, made before 1818, the road from Thealby to Crosby passed close to the elm trees, some of which still border the lawn on the west side of the Hall [in 1910]. This road was diverted near Normanby village and more acreage added to the Park about the time that the Hall was erected. It seems difficult to realize now that the main road from Normanby village to Crosby continued for a hundred yards within the iron gates before turning south to Crosby, and that considerable farm buildings occupied a position on the south side of the present approach.

Such was the story up to the year of Waterloo. Enter Sir Robert and then Robert Smirke. The two Roberts were to utterly transform the place, and lead the family and the Hall into the prosperous Victorian age.

The first Sir Robert had been born in Streatham on 25 February 1786, his mother being Penelope, the daughter of Sir Abraham Pytches, who himself had a grand home down in Streatham, a place called Mitcham Lane Manor House. His family had made their money through the vintner's trade in London, and he had five daughters. Penelope was the one who really gave the family a high profile connection. Abraham died in 1792, sure in the knowledge that his daughters were secure, and Penelope was Robert's bride just before Christmas 1818. Her husband was to take the Sheffields into the modern age, but he was also deeply attached to taking a firm hold of things in the homely status quo in North Lincolnshire.

Chapter 2

The Hall, the Park and Sir Robert

How wide the limits stand
Between a splendid and a happy land.
The Deserted Village, by Oliver Goldsmith

With Sir Robert Sheffield, the Fourth Baronet (who had a long spell in the seat of power, as he supervised the building of the new Hall in the 1820s and died in 1862), we are considering the life of a quintessential Victorian aristocrat/manager. Yes, he had helpers to administrate and he had tenant farmers to keep the production going, but he was the man at the helm. He shouldered all responsibility and the buck stopped at his door. He was a man of many talents and lived a life of profound service and dedication, serving as a magistrate as well, as so many landed gentry did. He fussed over details but had a clear vision for his domain, and he cared about people. Looking over his writings in the archives, the researcher cannot fail to be impressed.

There was to be a second nineteenth-century Sir Robert – his son – taking over the Hall and land. He died in 1886 after a worthy record in command. But Sir Robert the builder was, in many ways, the founding father of what Normanby was by the turn of the century, when Victoria's reign ended and the complexities of modernity brought wars and industrial upheaval.

The first Sir Robert was running the Hall and the lands with a working culture around him of that traditional rural identity we associate in popular imagery, art and literature: all the arts and crafts of village life, along with the farms, ploughmen and gardeners. The Normanby working estate was, under Sir Robert's guidance, a miniature empire. A glance at a census return for the mid-Victorian years tells us the infrastructure of that enterprise. In 1841 the listings for Normanby show agricultural labourers, gamekeepers, wheelwrights, apprentices, gardeners and, of course, the usual children, 'scholars', and the womenfolk.

The Normanby family had several estates, in the West and North Ridings of Yorkshire as well as Normanby itself; in the late eighteenth century, Charles Sheffield had sold off the last of the London property, and had to go to law in order to squeeze money out of John, Earl of Orrery, who owed him for property in Pimlico. That phase had garnered and gathered all the wealth, and now the family led a major agricultural workforce and land resource. Robert Sheffield set about being efficient and spent time in his library as well as out shooting or supervising others. At the basis of his work were his advice books.

The books were written during the late 1820s and up to 1838, when, as we shall see, he met with an accident that affected this activity. He listed the main categories of his notes and advice, and these were: estate improvements, cropping arrangements, timber sales, rabbits and other game, drainage of the Ancholme River, and estate plans. This was how he saw things around 1830. Before that, and before the new Hall was built, he had found time to do other things, such as enjoy the ceremonial life and social engagements of being High Sheriff of Lincolnshire, which he was in 1817.

Now, in the 1830s, he set about keeping matters under control. It has to be recalled that the decade of the 1830s – and in particular, the first five years – were very tough and testing times for rural England, and indeed for the towns; cholera struck many of the latter, and the former suffered all kinds of trouble, from arson attacks to riots, and at one point an epidemic of rural crime. Adrian Gray, who has written widely on Victorian crime, explains the Lincolnshire context:

In 1830–31 there had been an especially bad outbreak of incendiarism and rick-burning, part of which had been blamed on the mythical 'Captain Swing'. On 29 July 1831, Richard Cooling and Thomas Mottley were executed for a series of arson attacks on stacks and farm buildings in the Kirkby and Hagnaby district.... In December 1839, a farmer at South Thoresby was attacked. He lost a stack of wheat and two of oats valued at £250.

Sir Robert's land was not threatened or damaged in these ways, but the decade did not leave him unscathed, as will be made clear. But first, a look at his advice books will show what preoccupied him for most of his time. In the early 1820s, when things were more settled and peaceful around him, he fastened on everyday matters of profit, such as the timber resource:

> When timber is cut down, part of the tops [are] to be kept for making faggots for staithing [repairing river banks], which are requisite for that purpose, to be used with cliff stone. I find on further conference that it is not worthwhile to cut up the fills on the estate for stone for staithing but to buy and use cliff stone as is now the practice.

He also made extensive notes on minor but important details regarding every aspect of the land, such as the costs imposed for the use of gates in the park by farmers, or even this, which is practical advice for future Baronets: 'Bone in manure seems the answer, well as far as I can judge on this … two quarters of bone are for turnips.'

But there was also the main business – making money and dealing with tenants. Here, in early 1829, he sets out terms of use:

> Agreed with William Chatterton to have three fields on his farm this year on the following terms. The 3 fields on Low Tracehill from Pett Close – that is of the lambs at the end of the first season he is in the house. Two thirds of the expenses paid by the oncoming tenant. After the 2nd season, one half of this third; one third after 4th, one quarter on 5th year – clear again.

This is written down in such a way that we are following his thoughts as he tries to make clear for himself (and for the imagined reader) the niceties of such an agreement. It is so precise that it hints at either haggling or at a long-continued practice between the Hall and the tenants, something very specific and relating to margins of desired profit.

By the mid-1830s, he is reaching a point at which the work has gone on apace and he is aware of limits:

> I have now cut down so much timber since I began writing this book that it will not be desirable to cut any down before my son comes of age. This shameful matter … and with much attention in the will.

This seems to mean that he is making a resolution, and again, the thought of his future inheritor reading the notes creeps into his mind as he writes.

There is in Sir Robert's mind a constant sense of the need for order and routine. Supporting this is a logging of all events and accounting, as in his basic list of account books, which were kept by a man called Barker (estate manager):

1. Regular estate account balanced on the first of May annually.
2. Book of estate expenses, balanced monthly.
3. A book of the value and rentals of farms.
4. Timber book, giving an assessment of timber sold annually.
5. A crop book – showing the crops grown in different fields for many years.

Sir Reginald was keen to keep updating income and checking rentals. He repeatedly notes figures, such as 'rents of Normanby and Butterwick … 9,600'.

Then there are the large-scale practices of the time, explained in the notebooks too. These topics usually relate to profits, or efforts towards making more profits, such was the impetus for expanding margins and squeezing out everything that could be obtained from the land. Such a subject was warping, for instance. This was the action of flooding land with river water. It would lie for a while and the silt would permeate the soil, so increasing fertility. It appears to have begun in the early eighteenth century, when the waters of the Ouse and the Aire were so used at Rawcliffe.

Arthur Young, on his tour of the counties in the early nineteenth century, saw warping being undertaken at Morton, near Gainsborough. T.W. Beastall, in his history of agriculture in the county, explains that Young 'observed warping at Althorpe, Amcotts and Gainsborough. Warp could be carted and spread on sandy soil for turnips. It was claimed that it equalled dung in its effects.' The plans for the warping at Morton show that the work entailed making a warping drain from the Trent, and then cutting inlets from the drains; there had to be a warping sluice made at the cut from the river, and dams were used as each area was flooded for fertilization.

One of the most ambitious warpers in the area was Henry Healey, who owned a lot of land and also rented some, much of it bordering Sheffield land. Healey made huge investments in warping at Burringham, Ashby decoy and Crosby. Amazingly, as T.W. Beastall notes, he spent £31,760 on warping in the late 1820s and 1830s at Burringham and Ashby, and later he sold land to Charles Winn and to Sir Robert, as he switched to growing for a market in West Yorkshire.

According to some sources, warping was last practised in North Lincolnshire in 1867. Clearly, for Sir Robert, it was very much worthwhile, as he provided these figures in 1829: 'The following lands may be advantageously warped.' He listed eleven tenants, ending with this instance:

W. Scott: assessment – £201.18.9 … after warping – £535.10.0 … increased rent – £333.12.3.

Sir Robert was also very much interested in innovation, new ideas on farming generally, and in every snippet of information that might have some use. For instance, he kept a cutting from *The farmer's Journal* on the topic of 'using train oil as a steep for turnip seed'. Mr M Molditch of Thorney Fen, wrote:

I have every reason to believe that steeping turnip-seed twenty-four hours in train oil before sowing is as safe a prevention from the Fly as any expedient yet found, with as little trouble and expense. I will not be found [argued against] on what I here assert but I was complaining last summer to a friend of mine of the difficulty we laboured under from the Fly in getting into a crop of turnips. He said, 'Steep your turnips in train oil, a practice common in Lancashire … one quart of oil is sufficient for twenty bags of seed.

Whatever the efficacy of this practice, the point is that Sir Robert was interested, and no doubt he experimented with this. It was all about saving and making more money.

In fact, in the 1830s, crime was not the only issue for landowners. In 1836, the Tithe Commutation Act was passed. From early medieval times, one tenth of the produce on the land of a manorial estate was payable to the church. As early as 786 BC, this principle was agreed, and in 900 tithes became law. A rector could take all the tithes (and there were three kinds of tithes), and a vicar, just the small ones: they were split into great and small figures. But then, in 1836, it was enacted that payments of rents could substitute them. This brought about disputes across the land as landowners argued over payments to be paid.

The aim of the 1836 Act was expressed by John Meadows White, who was the solicitor in charge of creating the bill:

> The object of this Act is to convert all the uncommuted tithes in England and Wales into a corn rent-charge, payable in money according to the value of a fixed quantity of corn, as ascertained from year to year by the average price of corn for the seven years ending at the previous Christmas.

This is why the decisions of the Tithe Commission could be challenged, or at least appealed against, because the averages could be disputed. The government attempted to establish the average prices of wheat, corn and barley, and the Comptroller of Corns Returns, who was William Jacob from the years 1829 to 1835, and somehow, by arithmetic not entirely clear, ascertained for instance that the average price of wheat per quarter in 1835 was £39 4s.

It is hard for the modern reader to appreciate just how important tithes were for everyone with land, or who rented land. A work written at the time when tithes were still hotly disputed, *Key to the Tithe Question*, by the Reverend W.M. Hawkins (1887), explained for anyone interested the historical development of the system, and he put his finger on the very heart of the debate:

> Is it folly or wisdom to affirm that our ancestors – however pious – could possibly give to the church a tenth of things that had no existence? Such, for instance, as the skill of farmers and the labour of workmen, yet unborn, or of lands, that were then, and for hundreds of years afterwards, at the bottom of the sea. Is it sanity or insanity to affirm that any human beings had it in their power centuries ago to put a tax on all the agricultural capital of this age?

The Reverend Hawkins wrote the book to show that the 'ancients' had such power.

Sir Robert had tithes to pay on his land, of course, and smaller land renters or owners also had to pay. An example of a typical small-scale place is that of Hannah James of Flixborough, who had four areas that were productive and so subject to tithes. Her 'two cow gates', for instance, a pasture, brought in four guineas per annum, and her house and yard earned £5 9s. Altogether, her earnings came to £14 14s, and on top of that she paid a tithe of £2 14s. Sir Robert had these facts and figures, keeping an eye on all tenants, of course, and he noted about Hannah's place, 'This cottage well managed, would be full one shilling a day profit to a labourer.'

What about Sir Robert and his tithes? In 1849 he was haggling about payments due to the Commission for his 368 acres of land at West Butterwick. In one letter, which was written to an agent who was attending the Commission meetings for him, Sir Robert even went so far as to use two methods of arithmetical calculations to ascertain what amount he had to pay. One line of thought gave him a sum of £152, whereas another gave him £156 6s for the tithe due for Butterwick.

The entire process was slow and frustrating. A letter from a lawyer, John Collinson, in 1848, notes, 'We did not get through the tithe case.' Sir Robert, in reply to another statement of delay, wrote, 'I by your letter, will take any step not to admit to having that part of the West Butterwick land, valued on what the report stated.' What had happened was that a valuation had finally been given, and Sir Robert contested it in appeal. The result was a compromise, and an appeal report produced in October 1849 by Mr Rawlinson, for the Commission, stated that a few months before, a rent payment of £106 was given, and that was appealed. It was not good news for Sir Robert. A Mr Brown leased the land from Sir Robert, and someone called Atkinson had calculated that the new rent figure should be £106.

Mr Rawlinson gave a very different valuation:

perhaps £246 would be about the sum to take as the rent charge for West Butterwick with Kelfield on the principle adopted in the township of Owston but on looking through the items of Mr Atkinson's estimate I find that the quantity of land which he has assumed to be in wheat or potatoes is so much more considerable than was proved to be grown in the township and that no allowance has been made for wastes which must exist.

The tithe was due to be paid to the Archbishop of York, and so what emerges is a strange state of affairs. Land ownership often entailed a long leasehold from the Church of England, which had owned huge tracts of England for centuries. Tithes had been entrenched in the church law and in contracts. Sir Robert must have had a shock, but he would have found a way to make more profit somewhere else.

The tithe legislation created all kinds of problems and disputes. The Reverend Hawkins summed it all up in this way: 'This Act has cost the nation many a hundred thousand bright sterling!' He added that the salaries of the commissioners was about £26,000 a year, and the total administrative costs amounted to £34,000 a year.

Sir Robert married in December 1818, the bride being Julia Brigida, the daughter of Sir John Newbolt, who was Chief Justice out in Madras before returning in 1820 to Hampshire to be Chairman of the Quarter Sessions. Sir John had married Elizabeth Juliana Digby, and that lady was maid of honour to Queen Charlotte, so Sir Robert's wife had moved in high circles. Sir John had also been a close friend of George Canning, who was to become Prime Minister in 1827, and his contacts served him well, as he was given a job by Lord Chancellor Loughborough. He had also been MP for Bramber in 1800, and always seems to have landed very high status positions, including auditor of the Duchy of Lancaster. But later he was rather cold-shouldered, and it was thanks to Canning that he had the Madras appointment.

He was only 53 when he died in 1823, just five years after his daughter married Sir Robert.

Sir Robert and Julia were to have five sons and two daughters. The family man was always busy in public life though, and one of his main concerns was being Chairman of the Lindsey Quarter Sessions. At the time there was a house of correction in Kirton, and his Bench would have been composed of a circle of friends very much like himself. He served in that capacity for thirty years. As noted earlier in this chapter, rural crime escalated in the 1830s, but there was a steady stream of petty offences across Lindsey, and the magistrates were always busy. For instance, typical offenders were Thomas Hall, whose stole 50 feet of rope, and James Smith, of Gainsborough, who stone 5 stones of coal. Occasionally there were more serious offenders, as in the case of Charles Foreman, a labourer, working in tandem with Charlotte Foreman ('a single woman'); they were indicted for stealing 'one child's frock of the value of six pence, one child's petticoat to a value of six pence, three pairs of socks to the value of three pence … 10 yards of lace to the value of three shillings, one child's slip … and three pencil drawings.' These two were surely a regular little criminal enterprise.

Sir Robert had to witness, and give judgement on, some offences that highlight to the modern reader the often brutal and unfeeling nature of the criminal justice system in the mid-Victorian years. One such case was reported as being 'of revolting barbarity', when two men stood in the dock before the justices, having done what one reporter described as 'an act so barbarous as scarcely to be credited to having been perpetrated in Great Britain'. What happened was that the two men had followed and trapped a Winterton woman, and in a field they had forced her to strip. The victim, Sarah Neal, was in service to a local farmer, and she had an ordeal in court as well as in that field: 'She was put through a cross-examination of a very questionable kind from which it was attempted to be shown that she was in the family way, and she very modestly replied to the questions.'

The crime had been committed in October, in the early evening. The men gave her a greatcoat to wear for her walk home, which was a mile away. The men were transported for seven years. This came in 1851, just a few years before transportation to Australia stopped.

In the midst of that dour and dangerous decade, Sir Robert met with an accident while shooting, and this resulted in the loss of his right hand. This perhaps explains why the advice books come to a close at that time, 1836. But he still sat on the bench. Mixed in with the larceny and assault cases, there were broader, general issues concerning landed estates and crime. This meant poaching and all the confrontations and social oppositions associated with it. Over the centuries, poaching in England had often been regarded by many communities as a 'social crime' with the meaning that shooting and taking game or rabbits was an activity that would in many cases keep a labourer's family from starvation. The eighteenth century had brought a succession of Game Laws, all intended to protect the fowl and fauna on estates such as Normanby; the punishments were severe, as may be seen from a Lincolnshire case that is perhaps the most well known in the county from the Victorian period.

William Dadley was a young man from Aylsham in Norfolk who came to Lincolnshire and worked for Captain Mansell at Well Hall, near Alford. The prospects for a new life seemed good, and he married at St Botolph's church in Boston in January 1839, his bride being Margaret Brown. They planned to settle in a gamekeeper's house near Ulceby Cross. He was to work the area as Head Gamekeeper for a Member of Parliament, Robert Christopher. There he was, just married, and with a bright future to look forward to. The wedding celebrations began with a party on 10 January, but as the guests were having a good time, shots were heard out in the woods, and Dadley felt he had to go and investigate.

Strangely, though, he went out into the night unarmed, although he did take a man with him, Charles Harrison. There was a serious poaching problem on the estate; there had been recent prosecutions and the perpetrators sent to a house of correction, and some men had been given prison sentences. On this night, the young married man tracked down the poachers, but one of them turned on him and shot him dead.

There was one obvious suspect: a desperate character called John Baker from Partney, who was linked in some people's minds to another killing of a gamekeeper at Normanby. He had a reputation in the area for being a rebel and a dangerous man. There was a strenuous effort made to bring in Dadley's killer, and a reward was offered in the hope that someone would turn in the man responsible. All roads of enquiry did indeed lead to Baker, and he was arrested and charged, being hunted down to a village not far off, and cornered in a loft with a gun in his hand. Baker was faced with burglary charges as well, and was taken to Lincoln for trial. There was no definite evidence to convict him of the Dadley murder but he was convicted of serious theft charges and his sentence of death was commuted to transportation, as so many were at that time.

There is no certainty that Baker killed the young husband. It is not difficult to imagine the feelings about the sad affair in the area, and the headstone in the Well churchyard says something of this: it notes that he was 'hurried into his Redeemer's presence by the hand of a murderer, in the 32nd year of his age.' There is even a memorial stone in the place where he was shot, saying simply, 'W. Dadley murdered by poachers on this spot, 10 January 1839.'

The dark shadow of homicide associated with poaching reached Sheffield land. In December 1838, a watcher at the game preserve at the Park, Storey Jackson, was killed by a poacher. At the inquest, as the reporter from *The Morning Post* explained, one Edward Thompson told the coroner, Mr Marris, what had happened:

> About ten o'clock on Wednesday evening I and the deceased were employed together in watching the game preserves in Normanby Park. About twenty minutes before three o'clock on the morning of Thursday we heard the report of a gun in the direction of the fish-pond in the Park, when we immediately went to the place. A few seconds later we heard a second report of a gun about 30 yards from us, in the fish-pond plantation. The deceased and I then determined the one to go on one side of the plantation, and the other on the other. The deceased went to the east side. ... The deceased said to me 'They are here.' We then determined to jump over the paling ... and whilst we were getting over ... a person said ... 'Keep back or I will shoot you.'

Thompson went on, as did Storey Jackson, but Thompson fell down, while Jackson ran on. Thompson said he heard the voice of the shooter say, 'Stand back', and threaten to shoot again. But the poacher fired immediately after speaking, and Thompson heard Jackson go down, commenting that he 'gave a groan and expired instantly.' Thompson was then assaulted as he struggled to his feet, and he told the court, 'On raising myself again, I heard the person jump from the paling of the plantation, and the morning being dark, I saw no more of him.'

Thompson found a dead hen pheasant, and assumed that the poacher had shot this but left it. Another keeper, Isaac Chafer, came out, and he confirmed Thompson's statement that Jackson was dead at that time. The two keepers had been unarmed, carrying only sticks, and there appeared to have been only one poacher.

Poor Jackson was examined by a local doctor, Mr Des Forges, and he told the court that Jackson's left jaw was broken, and that the shot had penetrated his chest and lungs. There were no doubts as to the cause of death, but a verdict of accidental death was, rather strangely, returned. The hunt for the killer began, and there was a suspect. The first report of the inquest notes that a smock frock of the main suspect was in the hands of the local constable. Of course, there was no regional police force at the time, though that provision was to come in the near future.

Unfortunately, there is no satisfying conclusion to the story. All we have is an announcement in several county newspapers to the effect that a man suspected of being Jackson's killer had been arrested for a theft in Leicester.

On another Sheffield property, Lythe, in the North Riding of Yorkshire, just six years later, once again, a gamekeeper was murdered. This had been Earl of Mulgrave property since the time of James II. The head gamekeeper in 1844 was John Moffitt.

This turned out to be a significant case and trial, heard before the great judge, Mr Baron Rolfe, at York assizes: that of two rogues, George Lowther and Matthew Pearson, a labourer and a farm worker respectively, from the local area. In late January 1844, two watchers on the estate heard suspicious movements and they called for Moffitt, and another keeper, a Mr Wompra. There were altogether six men in the estate party, and they hid, waiting for the poachers to appear. They did so, and once again, as at Normanby, the estate men had no guns. When Moffitt called out to the two poachers, the intruders moved away, but Lowther threatened, 'Stand back or I'll blow your brains out!' Moffitt was deaf and he carried on in pursuit. He was mortally wounded by Lowther and he fell. The other keepers went in pursuit of Lowther and Pearson, and Lowther was caught. A report in a Whitby paper tells of the end of the events:

A constable went to the house where Pearson lived in Egton Green and found him there in great distress. Pearson told the constable where his gun was hidden. It was found there, loaded. Pearson was then taken to Mulgrave Castle and Moffitt died at 6 o'clock on the Tuesday evening. ... The case for Pearson's defence was that he had not taken any part in the shooting and had no intention of using his gun except for birds. The case for Lowther was that he had not shot Moffitt through premeditation. ... The jury found Lowther guilty and Pearson was acquitted.

Lowther was sentenced to hang, but this was commuted to transportation for life.

All this makes it clear that at this time the Normanby estates were, along with every other country house in the land, at the heart of rural crime, with clashes caused by poaching at the crux of the confrontations and deaths. These desperate encounters of poachers and keepers had been made much more potentially dangerous by legislation, because the 1862 Poaching Prevention Act had given police stop and search powers. As historian Alex Langlands explains:

This represented, in the eyes of Joseph Arch, an agricultural trade union leader giving evidence to a select committee on the Game Laws in 1873, a 'black day for the labourer' and an infringement of the basic liberty afforded to people of the labouring classes.

As we often find with criminal history, folklore tends to interfuse with the historical record, and Normanby is no exception. There is a tradition of a paranormal nature linked to the poaching days; it seems that there is a ghost known as Humphrey on the Sheffield land. Valerie Mercer recounted the tale for me:

The poor man was caught poaching on Sheffield land, and the gamekeeper and his cohorts attacked him, resulting in his death. The story goes that ever after, this man haunts the area where he was killed ... which became Lysaghts steelworks. He was known as Humphrey and many steelworkers have sworn they have seen him while they were working.

There are certainly plenty of incidents in the records regarding poaching offences. By 1862 (the year of the aforementioned Act), just a few months before the death of Sir Robert, a group of keepers had caught two poachers from Ashby, by the use of nets and two dogs. Matters had clearly become more efficient in that respect since the 1830s.

Sir Robert continued, busy as ever in spite of his lost hand, for many years. The income to maintain the home and family came from a variety of sources, so there was always paperwork and administration to control. Apart from rents and income from sales, there were such sources as neighbouring owned land. At nearby Flixborough, for example, as one writer in 1922 noted:

> Its parish contains 211 souls and 2,355 acres of land, partly in rich marshes near the river. Sir Robert Sheffield is owner of the soil, lord of the manor and patron of the church ... and the united benefices are now valued at £752 per annum.

When he did turn his thoughts towards the security of what he had (which was all the time, of course), the details of the insurance give the modern reader a keen sense of monetary values of that time. In 1836, for instance, the insurance for the house against loss or damage by fire cost £3 15s. In the policy we have some fine detail that gives insights into the material nature of the place: 'A dwelling house and office adjoining and communicating therewith, brick built and stated called Normanby Hall and situated at Burton Stather in the County of Lincoln ... five thousand pounds ... a warm air stove therein allowed.'

In practical, everyday terms, the Hall and its tenants needed machines and tools; throughout Sir Robert's long tenure as head of the family and Hall, agricultural change and advancement in Britain was marked by the improvements in farm machinery and transport, and the Normanby farmers and the estate manager at the Hall, as well as Sir Robert himself, would have kept pace with this revolution in technology. Down the road from Normanby, in the village of Winterton, for instance, there was the firm of John Fletcher. In 1863, an advert in a county directory shows Fletcher's handbill describing a 'new, improved, combined reaping and mowing machine'. They also provided 'Combined steam threshing machines, portable and fixed; all kinds of corn, seed and tillage drills, straw cutters, corn grinders, turnip cutters, cake breakers, horse hoes, Healey's patent turnip Fly and caterpillar destroyers'.

John Fletcher, founder of the company, had set up the Newport Ironworks in Winterton. He had at first teamed up with his first employer, Beacock, who was a typical example of a Victorian inventor and man of business. He would have dealt with the estate workers and foremen in the Hall workshops and stores in Normanby village. Charles Parker, historian of the firm, gives one example of Fletcher's activities:

> In 1855, John Fletcher designed a horse-drawn grass-mower that used the principle of a blade reciprocating over a series of fixed fingers, and in 1864 he took out a patent for a renewable ledger plate for the fixed fingers' cutting edge.

So, there was new technology, and also a development in the nationally based support organizations for landowners and farmers, notably, the Royal Agricultural Society (RAS). This had been formed by private individuals in 1838, and then given its charter in 1840. A principal aim was the application of science, and a perfect instance of this is recorded in the diaries of the novelist and estate owner Rider Haggard in 1898, in which the 'new man' of the country clashes with the economist:

> Today I received the report of the analyst on the stomach of the foal, which I sent to him to be examined. It is a negative document. For he can tell us nothing of the cause of death beyond that it was probably brought about by a vegetable poison, very violent, of which we were already convinced. What is not negative is his bill.

Nevertheless, the RAS did have large-scale involvement from people such as Rider Haggard and Sir Robert. Joining professional and scholarly societies was just one of many activities Sir Robert participated in. There was a North Lincolnshire Agricultural Society also, and a typical event was the 1856 exhibition of stock. This was in Market Rasen, and it was a precursor of the now very popular Lincolnshire Show, held north of Lincoln every June. It was very impressive, as one newspaper reported:

About one-third of the field was appropriated to the display of the implements, which were 112 in number, and the proportions of original designs or improvements during the year would bear comparison with those of any county association that we are acquainted with.

It was a swell occasion, and Sir Robert was relaxing with most of his county fellow land owners. The report notes that the dinner took place 'in a pavilion acknowledged by all to be far superior to anything of the kind which the Society had ever used'.

The Lincolnshire Agricultural Society was formed in 1796, and by 1819, when Sir Robert was in control at the Hall, the city of Lincoln paid for a second show to be established. But there had been one nearer home for the Hall, as the North Lincolnshire Society (NLS) held its first show in 1837 at Brigg. We have a good idea of what the NLS meetings were like in the early years (the 1840s) from the newspapers. The reports were not always positive, as in this: 'There was a moderate lot of horses, Mr T. Heseltine won the whip given by Lord Worsley for the best hunting colt; he was a very moderate one and not deserving it.'

Later in the century, as will be seen, the second Sir Robert, and then Sir Berkeley, were to play a much more prominent part in the county shows. After all, these were the best opportunities to show off and have a 'good press' across the county.

Sir Robert was also, along with all his confreres, very much politically oriented. One of the most pervasive and significant phases of political life in Sir Robert's time was Protectionism. This doctrine relates to the economic notion that foreign imports, competing with home-produced goods, must be regulated and have duties imposed, in order to safeguard domestic products. There were regular meetings across the county on this, at which speakers had their say, and the events were well attended. Sir Robert was present at a meeting in Lincoln in 1850. *The Illustrated London News* produced a drawing of the event, with fisticuffs breaking out in the gallery and on the floor. But we have to ask what the truth of the occasion was, because a Mr Cracroft, who was present, wrote, 'Everyone, even that scoundrel, Mr John Norton, had the most patient hearing given him ... proceedings were a pattern of respectability.'

It was a frame of mind against the grain in the mid-Victorian period, as reforms were gradually made in the spirit of free trade. From 1842 to 1845, Sir Robert Peel reduced or abolished duties on a number of raw materials. In 1846, the Corn Laws were repealed and so free trade was becoming widespread in commerce with Europe and the countries outside the Empire. Then, in 1860, Gladstone abolished all duties on fruit and dairy produce.

At that time, the farmers were influential in politics in the rural world around Normanby. By the time of the second great Reform Act of 1867, farmers with 30 acres and more had the vote; they composed one tenth of the county population, but formed half of the electorate at the time of the Lincoln meeting, so it comes as no surprise to learn that 3,000 such small farmers from the Isle of Axholme (which is close to Normanby land) attended.

It is not difficult to imagine the Normanby estate, circa 1850. There would be Sir Robert, the paterfamilias of the family, the man at the very core of the property, land and people. Around him there would be his children, busy being educated at the best places; the middle management men, supervising and planning; the servants in the Hall and the array of manual workers keeping the productivity high, always working long hours, and knowing their place in the hierarchy of the class structures at the heart of the land and the Empire. This would be replicated across the country. It was a workable system, paternalistic and steady, conservative and cautious, but always upholding the kind of vision we find in Lord Tennyson's poem *Ulysses* – a poem that appealed to the progressive Victorians, with the lines:

> *that which we are, we are;*
> *One equal temper of heroic hearts,*
> *Made weak by time and fate, but strong in will,*
> *To strive, to seek, to find, and not to yield.*

During the mid-Victorian years, there was another side to the Normanby enterprise. To look at this we need to switch focus to the great Victorian project of bringing basic education to the working class. The key figure in this story is the Reverend Charles Sheffield, the son of Sir Robert, Third Baronet, who married Sarah Ann Kennet after the death of his first wife,

Penelope Pitches, as related earlier in the chapter. Sir Robert and Sarah had their son Charles and six daughters. Sarah's life was rather tinged with scandal, or at least notoriety, because her grandfather was Brackley Kennet, the Lord Mayor of London from 1779 to 1780, and in office when the horrendous 1780 Gordon Riots took place. He did not handle the tumult very well, as he failed to read the Riot Act and did not arrange protection to the vulnerable areas of the city, the Catholic people. The rogue who led the incursions, Lord George Gordon, was spurred into violence by the concessions that had been made to Catholics. The result was that 135 people were tried and twenty-six hanged, and the army had fired at the mobsters and killed several of them.

The Reverend Charles Sheffield became Vicar of Flixborough. He was keen to have an elementary school at Burton-upon-Stather, and approached the Incorporated National Society, which had been formed in 1811. Its full name, by the time the Reverend Sheffield was in touch with them in 1846, was The National Society for Promoting the Education of the Poor in the Principles of the Established Church. The theory behind the organization came from the teachings of Dr Bell, who created the monitorial system. This was a method in which the teacher taught material to a small group, and these became monitors who passed it on to other pupils.

By the 1830s, the government was giving grants to the National Society, although with the cash came inspections, as always seems to be the case. Whatever shortcomings we perceive in this approach today, it appealed to the Reverend Sheffield. In 1846 he received a grant of £30 for his school from the National Society, and the small print gives a clear account of what was wanted. For instance, there is this, defining what is asserted regarding the new school: 'That the new school house … is finished in a satisfactory and workmanlike manner, being built of proper dimensions and fully completed in all respects according to the statement forwarded to the Society.'

A trust deed was made and executed, and the stipulations regarding the rationale for the teaching were absolutely clear, in six statements, the principle one being: 'The children are to be instructed in the Holy Scriptures and in the Liturgy and Catechism of the established Church.' Of course, being part of a national system, the process had to involve reports, to be made every Christmas and sent to the Diocesan Board, the District Society or the National Society.

Soon, the Reverend Sheffield was ordering materials, including 100 slate pencils, at a cost of 2s 6d, and '100 reward cards for good behaviour', costing 7s. Parochial copy books were ordered, along with 'first maps' and elementary copy books. The Reverend Sheffield was a busy man, travelling around the area to advance the work. His expenses detail everything from 'timber felling' to travel, which included himself and his sons. For instance, at one point he went to York, noting that he must have been at a school there. Perhaps he was watching and learning. Whatever the reason, he claimed '3 days at 4s ... 12s', and for 'son Joseph ... 8 ditto at 3/6 ... 12.0.7d'.

There had been some assistance from Sir Robert, which included voluntarily giving a small piece of land at Burton as the site for the school. True to form, even that brought costs: it involved the execution of deed and a fee to the Master in Chancery, along with time spent in Chancery, and the agent's fee for writing a deed.

There was cash in every corner of life, and in the first Sir Robert's reign, he had shown himself to be a master of administration, overlooking everything and missing nothing.

Sir Robert died in November 1862. The largest county paper stated the bare facts, and added that he was 'chairman of the Kirton Quarter Sessions, and Deputy Lord Lieutenant of Lincolnshire', and that he was succeeded by his son, Robert, who had been a captain in the Royal House Guards. The next Robert Sheffield was about to take his place in the Hall.

Chapter 3

The Second Sir Robert and Sir Berkeley

Business was his pleasure; pleasure was his business.
The Contrast, by Maria Edgworth

In 1886, Sir Robert Sheffield was following in his father's footsteps. The local directory lists him under Winterton as the principal magistrate. The village, which is a few miles along to the east, further from the Humber than Burton, then had a population of 1,601 and an area of 3,628 acres. Nothing much had changed since Sir Robert's father had sat on the bench for Kirton, a little further away. But he must have felt the satisfaction that he was a proper Sheffield. He had been as busy as his father since his taking over, and within a few years of his regime at Normanby there were great changes afoot in agriculture.

In 1872, the acreage of tillage was in decline, and this steadily continued into the next century. In that same year, the first trade union for farm workers was created, led by Joseph Arch. The signs of the times hit North Lincolnshire, and this is evident in the press report on the Elsham and Worlaby Cottagers' Agricultural Show in 1874, at which Sir Robert was present. This was:

The cottagers have evidently been incited to compete with each other by the annual exhibitions of this society which, therefore – notwithstanding its provision complained of in the Daily News, *that 'No person in the Agricultural Labourers' Union, on or after 1 of June 1874, will be allowed to compete in this show' – may be said to be doing a useful and praiseworthy work.*

But apart from such disputes, the new Sir Robert carried on as he was traditionally supposed to do, attending shows and dinners, sitting on the magistrate court bench and making sure that he was seen to be doing philanthropic work in the locality. In November 1865, for instance, he saw the opening lecture given at the reading room and library he had established at Burton-upon-Stather: this was a talk given by the Reverend Charles Sheffield on 'Manners and Customs of our Aristocratic Forefathers'. In 1866, he killed a stag weighing 15 stones while in a shooting party at Glanavon, the estate of the Duke of Richmond, who was, incidentally, a powerful presence in Sir Robert's old regiment, the Royal Horse Guards. He chaired the meeting of the Horse Guards' command at Knightsbridge Barracks in 1871. Such was the network of friends and contacts around the Sheffields, as with all their counterparts in the other estates.

Sir Robert had joined the Horse Guards as cornet in 1842, when he was just 19, progressing to the rank of captain in 1849. In January 1867, he married Priscilla, the third daughter of Colonel Harry Dumaresq, who had served in the Crimean War, and who served with the Royal Engineers until he retired in 1882. Harry Dumaresq's life deserves a biography to itself. He was born in 1792, and by 1817 he was a lieutenant colonel. In *A New Biographical Dictionary*, by Hugh James Rose, we have this staggering account of Harry's deeds:

> He entered the army at the age of 16, and served in eight campaigns, of which six were in the Peninsula, one in Canada, and the last, that of Waterloo. He was present in the thirteen battles for which medals were bestowed, besides many affairs of outposts, of advance and rear guards, also at the Siege of Badajoz and Burgos, and at the assault of the fortress of Salamanca.... He was employed on the staff of command for eighteen years.... He was twice dangerously wounded. At the Battle of Waterloo he was on the staff of Lieutenant General Sir John Byng. He was the officer of whom the following anecdote is told by Sir Walter Scott ... amid the havoc which had been made among his immediate attendants, His Grace sent off an officer to a general of the brigade in another part of the field; in returning he was shot through the lungs, but as if supported by the resolution to do his duty, he rode up to the Duke of Wellington, delivered the answer to his message, and then dropped off his horse, to all appearance a dying man.

Harry (properly, Henry) married Elizabeth Danvers in 1828 at St George's, Hanover Square, London. At Elizabeth's death in 1877, she left their daughter Priscilla the huge sum of £5,000.

The other Dumaresq connection is that of Harriette, who was born in New South Wales in February 1828, and married Rowland Winn in March 1854. We will meet Rowland again in chapter 7.

Robert and Priscilla's first son, the future Sir Berkeley, was born on 24 January 1876. In 1880 there had been a desperately tense time, when Lady Priscilla fell seriously ill while abroad. *The Hull Packet* reported:

Lady Sheffield, sister of Mr Rowland Winn … is very ill in Homburg. Last week diphtheria was feared, and her sister, Mrs Constable, was telegraphed for from England, and Lady Sheffield is now, it is hoped, recovering from this alarming attack.

She did recover, living on until 1900.

Sir Robert's public life went from strength to strength, as he was as committed to good work as his father had been. By 1868, he was sitting on the Brigg Board of Guardians, and two years later, was nominated as a sheriff of the county; throughout their history, the Sheffields had, naturally, married into the people in the regional power base as a matter of course. Julia Sheffield, for instance, daughter of the first Sir Robert, married Sir John Trollope, who was to become Lord Kesteven in 1868. Trollope had been High Sheriff of Lincolnshire and was MP for Lincolnshire South in 1841. He and Julia had three sons and three daughters.

In the early years, the children's education entailed private schooling. There were academies springing up everywhere in the Victorian mid-century era. The Chestnut House Academy in Arnold, Nottingham, was favoured by Sir Robert, and in the advertisement for the school at the time, both Rowland Winn and Sir Robert are named as referees. It was an interesting place: for many years it was managed by Joseph Phipps, who was very keen on science education and was noted for his experiments as part of the curriculum. His alumni included John Robinson, future High Sheriff of Nottinghamshire, and the apothecary Joseph Townend, who emigrated to New Zealand and made a name for himself.

In *Morris's Directory* for 1844, it is described as 'an excellent private school' and in a later edition of the same, the facilities are described. These included a gymnasium 'fitted with all requisite apparatus' and 'a new and capacious lecture and recreation hall, 36 feet by 17 feet', along with 'hot and cold water baths'. We know that in 1871, Phipps had thirty-eight pupils. Overall, it appears to have offered a traditional curriculum, but with the addition of the more modern element of scientific knowledge – and that was a feature that would attract the wealthy Victorians.

In the late Victorian years, the higher journalism liked to stir things up regarding the aristocracy, and the gossip columns and footnotes in such periodicals as *The Pall Mall Gazette* were always likely to have something to say that would provoke thought and discussion in the chattering classes. In 1869, for example, this little paragraph would very likely have disturbed Sir Robert over his breakfast:

> Taking the extinct peerages of England first – the Sheffields, Dukes of Buckingham and Normanby, were descended from Sir Robert Sheffield, of the Inner Temple, Knight, Recorder of London and Speaker of the House of Commons in the reign of Henry VIII, which Sir Robert … very much advanced and purchased a fair estate in the county of Lincoln … and Sir Robert Sheffield, the illegitimate descendent of John, first Duke of Buckingham and Normanby, is now in possession.

That little footnote in the genealogy – the assumption of the title by Charles Sheffield, the half-brother of Edmund, who became the First Baronet, was always going to be a slight irritation.

But Sir Robert and Lady Priscilla were immensely popular, and some of the best testaments to this are found in the piles of ephemera that have survived, such as a poem especially written for their return to the Hall after the birth of Berkeley in 1876, written by one Charles Clay of Messingham. The verse includes these lines:

> *Nine years ago took place we know, Sir Robert's wedding day;*
> *Crowds flocked to see – at Appleby – Miss Dumaresq given away;*
> *Claimed equal rank, firm as the Bank, is scarce to find on earth*
> *A better man, say what you can, a gentleman from birth.*

Chorus: *Now welcome back to Normanby, Sir Robert and his Lady fair,*
Long may they live, advice to give, to their first-born son and heir!

It has been noted that when Priscilla was ill, she was in Homburg, and that German town was one of the Prince of Wales's favourite spots when he wanted to indulge his instinct for pleasure to the full. He had often been seen there, usually gambling, and this was reported in the British press. Jane Ridley, Edward's biographer, gives us a clear sense of the attractions of Homburg for him:

At Homburg in 1882, Bertie's list of dinner guests included an American family: Mr, Mrs and Miss Chamberlain. Nineteen-year-old Jane Chamberlain was the daughter of William Selah Chamberlain, millionaire heir to a Cleveland railroad fortune. A shrewd American debutante, she refused to see Bertie without her parents being present. 'Chamberpots', as Alix [the prince's wife] called her, remained in favour for a couple of years.

The fact that Priscilla spent time in Homburg is significant with regard to one episode in her life that gave her a place in a major scandal – the matrimonial suit of Lord Durham. This was in 1885, and lady Sheffield was called to give testimony in court with reference to Lord Durham's wife, whose maiden name had been Ethel Milner. She had been a friend of Priscilla's, and reading between the lines, we may see that many aristocratic ladies such as those two spent time in such places as Homburg, enjoying more restrained pleasures while their husbands were at the gaming table or, in some cases, entertaining mistresses. It is clear from the now voluminous body of writing about Victorian marriages of wealthy and titled people that keeping mistresses was the norm. Marriage was not necessarily about sexual pleasure, but about ensuring children. This is where the case of Lord Durham's matrimonial suit entered life and conversation at Normanby.

This suit began in early 1885, before Sir James Hannen, and it was a suit in which Lord Durham sued for the annulment of his marriage to Ethel on the grounds of her insanity.

Several ladies were called in order to ascertain whether or not Ethel was insane. One witness stressed that there was never anything to suggest that the woman was 'at all defective in intellect'. After a visit to Cannes, one witness noted, Ethel became more 'gushing' and looked 'pale'. Lady Sheffield was then called, and *The Standard* reported:

> Lady Sheffield was the next witness called, and examined by the Attorney General. She said, 'I am the wife of Sir Robert Sheffield. I have known Lady Durham ever since she was born.'

She was asked how she would describe Ethel, and she replied:

> She was a most happy child, and took part in all childish play. As she grew up she became more shy, but she was still a very pleasant girl. I saw Lady Durham in the summer of 1882. She stayed with me some time. I reminded her of some stories from her childhood, about her dressing up in character and so on. She enjoyed them very much and entered into the fun of them. She drove out with me on various occasions. I saw her in London after her engagement to Lord Durham.

Here was Lady Sheffield doing a very effective job of showing that her friend Ethel was normal, and had no impairments of mind. She had stressed her humour and her ability to communicate well. When asked if Ethel was 'sensible', she replied, 'Very much so. She was decided in her opinions, and expressed them clearly. I was not present at her marriage but I saw her after.' The prosecutor really pressed for some kind of statement that might back up the insanity allegation. He asked Lady Sheffield if she had any inklings of such traits, and she replied, 'I never did. I always considered her an intelligent, sensible girl.'

As another paper reported when the case was concluded later, there was something other than questions of insanity: 'The conduct of Lady Durham after the engagement was evidence of want of affection; but where he found want of affection he found no want of sanity.' After the visit to Cannes, which had been considered as a turning point of some kind, this allegedly led to her deterioration. No less a person than Sir William Gull was called to speak. He was a Royal Physician and had begun to specialize in female illnesses such as the malaise we now call anorexia. He said that he saw no evidence of insanity.

The petition was dismissed with costs, but that was not the end of it. A man of money and power wanted Ethel out of the way, and her destiny was to spend most of her life in what they would then refer to as a 'mental home'. She came out into society shortly before her death in 1931.

The whole affair showed upon the woeful lack of knowledge of mental illness at that time. In the criminal law there was just as much confusion and prejudiced thinking as in the civil law; there had been a Lincolnshire case, for instance, in which a man had been condemned to die for murder, when in fact he had been suffering from a fit. But in the civil and church courts there was a steady stream of cases involving the failed marriages of the wealthy. Lady Sheffield had played a strong and admirable role in speaking for common sense in a closed-in world of wealth and status, in which it was a very easy matter for an 'inconvenient' person to be removed from the family.

As for Sir Robert, he was carrying on as normal while this scandal was filling the national newspapers. For instance, he was at the petty sessions and sitting on the bench, as his father had done, listening to cases of small thefts and assaults. In August 1885, he had this list of offences before him: cruelty to a horse by a Scunthorpe man; use of a cart without a name on it; riding without reins; cruelty to a pony; and disorderly conduct.

Around that time also, there was a typical election experience for Sir Robert. Through the nineteenth century, electoral meetings were notoriously violent and noisy, and at Scunthorpe there was exactly such an event, called by the local paper 'a discreditable radical rowdyism'. This was when James Lowther MP was supposed to be making a farewell speech. The Sheffields were at the very epicentre of a virtual riot, as this report described:

It has been indicated that the concerted and studied insult of the local Radicals noisily manifested itself when some of Mr Lowther's friends, including Sir Robert and Lady Sheffield, Colonel Dumaresq and Mrs Dumaresq, Mr Goulton Constable and Mrs Goulton Constable, and Mr Hugh Inglis came on the platform. The noise became intensified as the chairman and Mr Lowther made their appearance, and when

Mr Dove rose for the purpose of introducing Mr Lowther, the insane sibilation, whistling and groaning were redoubled.

Lowther did try to speak, but herrings were pelted at the platform. The meeting was abandoned, and the Lowther party went to the Blue Bell inn for dinner, but there was still a noisy mob outside as they tried to escape the stress and clamour of that hateful meeting.

Now we should come down to earth, as it were, and consider the actual land itself. I have said nothing yet about the gardens at the Hall at this time, before the turn of the century, and the development of all the resources of the Hall and its grounds in a variety of ways. Basically, as with almost every country house in the land, as we have seen from the first Sir Robert's advice books, not a square foot of soil was wasted, and in true Victorian fashion, everything was used, whether it was sourced from beasts, plants, soil or water. In the mid-century, when the gardens, for instance, were receiving constant attention, there was an important source of knowledge in the family itself – the Earl of Ilchester, who had married Sir Robert's daughter in 1857.

He was a great horticulturalist, and as his obituary noted, 'Since his retirement he devoted a great deal of attention to the culture of flowers and plants and his gardens at Abbotsbury [Dorset] bear evidence of the care and attention bestowed upon them.' He was a remarkable man in many ways. He built a number of model cottages for labourers, for instance, and was known as a generous and kind-hearted man. One may sense his presence when contemplating the walled garden at the Hall. Imagining the conversation at dinner about cultivating pear trees or choosing a variety of potato to grow is surely not too fanciful.

Visiting the walled garden today, it is an invitation to imagine the place in its heyday, when the head gardener ruled supreme and a gang of minions followed his directions down to every small detail. The successful cultivation of plants for the table at the Hall was essential. As David Taylor stressed in his book on the Hall between the world wars:

The head gardener was usually a married man, and lived in the first cottage on the right on the road to Burton in Normanby village. He was an important figure in the running of the estate, ranking alongside the clerk of works, the head gamekeeper and the head woodman in seniority. This was sufficient for him to have his name listed in Kelly's commercial directory for Lincolnshire.

The Victorian garden in this context, of the first Sir Robert's time, formed the template for succeeding years: the land itself was methodically marked out and plants allotted after much thought and planning.

The area itself, still seen clearly today, was created in 1817, and was part of the rebuilding notions of the first Sir Robert. It has been noted how frugal and circumspect he was in business dealings and in domestic economy, and this attitude is also observed in the garden. It developed as a crucially important part of the estate, and over the years, the figure for the number of staff employed ranges from eleven to eight. Later, towards the end of the nineteenth century, the man who ran the gardens was Ernest Allen, who had started work there in 1876, destined to follow his brother Henry, who was the head gardener for much of the first Sir Robert's time there.

The estates up and down the land, since the Renaissance, had not embellished their lands simply by any passing whim. As the cultural historian Michael Pye puts it,:

Gardens and parks no longer made some vast general claim about man's ability to dominate and remake the world around him. They made smaller, local statements about their owners, with an inordinate amount of heraldry in the shaping of stones and beds to proclaim names, ancestry, rank and connections. They were like the detail of a clever machine.

The gardens were also about order and rationality. The great age of 'Improvement' in the Regency period had made celebrities of landscape builders such as Humphrey Repton. In her novel *Mansfield Park*, Jane Austen makes very effective fictional use of the notion of 'improving' one's land. Mrs Norris (the aunt of main character Fanny Price) expresses a common view of the time:

But if dear Sir Thomas were here, he could tell you what improvements we made. ... We were always doing something. ... It was only the spring twelvemonth before Mr Norris's death we put in an apricot against the stable wall.

Austen is having fun with the innovation on country estates, merely for the vogue.

In the social calendar of the year for English aristocrats, events followed (and still follow) the 'season' in which certain pursuits take place by tradition. Consequently, a very important phase of life was the autumn shooting season, through to Christmas. But garden produce was not only expected to be there to sustain the family at that obviously active and busy time. No; there was a family address in London too, and they often holidayed in Scotland, near Loch Morar, and so hampers were made and the garden produce went with them on their journeys.

We have a glimpse of the planning involved in the records of the gardeners. For instance, in 1903, one entry notes, 'Seeds sown'. This listing shows the sound basis of knowledge behind the work: 'Bed of onions, Ailsa Craig, Veitch's maincrop, Veitch's selected globe, Suttons long-keeping, Suttons Perfection Giant ... well manured and soot and super phosphorus lightly forked in and well rolled before seed.'

The work put into gardening was staggeringly impressive. Phil Lusby, of the Royal Botanic Garden in Edinburgh, told one writer recently for a feature in *The Scotsman*,: "'I think it's their sheer hard work that leaves you speechless," says Phil ... Loudon [the famous Scottish botanist] himself had his right arm amputated but he still wanted to carry on gardening the same day.'

As a guide to the walled garden provided for visitors to the Hall makes clear, there were sound and sensible reasons for the positioning of the various plants in the large rectangular area. The plot was in quarters, and there were vegetable borders on three sides, with a peach case, vinery and vinery beds on the other side. At the West Wall there was a cut flower and herb border, and a path cut across the beds.

Back in about 1860, this overall standard design accommodated a number of other products, such as cherries, plums and currants (grapes), and of course there were a number of long frames for more delicate fruits. In addition, the walls were made in such a way that the south facing wall would have most sunshine and the north and south walls were longer than the others. This thinking was well established; in 1724, a writer called Stephen Switzer had worked out this kind of planning, and wrote that a south wall that slanted at 20 degrees would experience the best air – the clear morning air, rather than the hotter afternoon air.

The greenhouses were important too. Over the centuries, such places had been kept warm with the use of stoves, before they were exclusively made of glass. But in 1845 there was a repeal of the Glass Tax, and so greenhouses as we know them emerged and became common. Heating them was a challenge, and at first this entailed the use of a fire, and water pipes came later.

There was a range of technology in use as well, to support the work done. For instance, items such as syringes and hosepipes would be needed, as well as such marvels as Green's garden engine. Naturally, the world of commerce was alert to all this, and the press was sprinkled with adverts for such things as oil engines, cake nuts and meals, hothouses, frames and plant houses. 'Anco', for instance, promoted their products with these large claims: 'ANCO products are carefully and scientifically compounded from the soundest and best ingredients only. They are extremely digestible and give the very best returns for money spent.'

The notion of the walled garden goes back a long way; even in works from ancient civilizations there are accounts of such things, and as usual, the Victorians gave much thought to their use. As the authors of the television series *Victorian Farm* explain:

By this period, so wide was the range of fruits, vegetables and herbs grown that gardens became compartmentalized. These gardens that had no room to cater for new interesting plants and innovative techniques were moved to more suitable locations and often set a distance away from the country house so that their increasingly industrial character did not offend its residents.

Consequently, there was something akin to the old medieval monastic garden in this cultivation. The monasteries had prominent herb and fruit gardens, and many of the skills and traditions involved in those were perpetuated in the Victorian era.

Then there were the staff – the hierarchy of garden workers. In the later Victorian years, the crock boy, who mostly cleaned and looked after pots, was at the bottom, earning one shilling a day, up to the head gardener, who was essentially a supervisor, and he would earn close on £80 a year. As literature produced about the Hall for visitors makes clear, in those last decades of the nineteenth century, there were eleven people employed to work the gardens. In addition to the long greenhouse, there were all kinds of other outbuildings as well, ranging from a bothy or mess room, down to a pot store.

From the walled garden out to the deer park and the tenant farms, and from the village workshop in Normanby itself out to the land at Flixborough by the Trent, the huge domain of the Sheffields was always impressive. Today, if the visitor walks up the slope of what is known as Ackie's Warren (after Walter Atkinson, the estate gamekeeper, whose story will be told in the next chapter) they will see from the top the vista of the Trent and Flixborough to the west, and Normanby to the east. On those heights now there are residual mounds of slag from the former ironworks at Lysaghts, which was the closest plant in the once gargantuan spread of steel making around Scunthorpe. But to look across that open vista is to appreciate just how much land was under the responsibility of the Normanby workers and managers.

Sir Robert died on 23 October 1885, and in his will (made in 1884) he left his widow Priscilla as sole executrix, with a personal estate of more than £19,000, which we have to multiply by about fifty to have today's value. The real estate was left to their son, Berkeley George Digby. Then began the long tenure of Sir Berkeley Sheffield, a man whose life and work are much more detailed and well known in the villages that cluster around Scunthorpe; by the time he gathered new resources and made material changes to the Hall and estate, the age of the popular press had really arrived, and the media took much more interest in the affairs of local dignitaries. In addition, there was the fact that Sir Berkeley was very much involved in local politics, as will be explained later in the chapter.

Sir Berkeley's employment of Walter Brierley brought notable changes to the Hall. The *Country Life* feature of 1911 called attention to the challenge that the new architect faced:

It is obviously a very difficult problem to add to a building designed by Smirke a wing which shall stand confessed as a work of the present day, while yet presenting a not too violent contrast with the subtle refinements of the older building.

But the writer was pleased with the result.

Walter Brierley was born in 1862, and worked as an architect based in York for many years, being the architect for the whole diocese of the city. During the forty years following 1885, he worked on no less than 300 buildings, ranging from several schools (many in York), to Northallerton County Hall and Borough Court in Leicester. He started his career in partnership with James Demaine at York, and then later, James Rutherford. The *Country Life* writer of 1911 was impressed by the work, which was mainly the addition of large servants' quarters, built at the back of the Hall. The writer noted:

The new servants' quarters are masked to a large extent on the garden side by the projecting wing, and at the approach by large shrubberies, so they have been built in red brick with stone dressings instead of entirely in stone. In the inside of the house Mr Brierley naturally allowed himself a freer hand than outside, and no doubt Smirke would be very astonished at the plaster ceilings in the dining room and elsewhere.

This new wing was to last until 1949, when it was demolished.

Walter Brierley died in 1926. He had been truly indefatigable; in addition to all the country houses, he also worked on racecourse architecture, being responsible for the complete remodelling of the famous Rowley Mile stand at Newmarket, and for improvements at the Knavesmire, the York racecourse. His obituary in *The Times* summed him up: 'He worthily maintained the dignity of his profession, and was in the forefront with those who strive to uphold and elevate the standards of its aims and achievements.'

On 19 July 1904, Sir Berkeley married Julia, Baroness de Tuyll, who was just twenty-one; they married in The Hague. The Tuyll family is a noble Dutch family, with the full title of Van Tuyll van Serooskerken. They claim their descent from an ancient family, being traceable as far back as 1125. By the eighteenth century, many in their ranks had achieved distinction, notably in the arts and in the history of ideas. Isabelle van Tuyll (1740–1805), for instance, was a writer. Later, some distinguished themselves in the army, and then in 1822, there was a significant event in the genealogy: the High Council of Nobility confirmed that the van Tuylls were entitled to be defined as being in the highest rank of nobility. Links with Britain began to be formed, as in General Sir William Tuyll, who became a Knight of the Bath and aide de camp to the Marquess of Anglesey.

Carel van Tuyll was a traveller and explorer, and working with the Prince of Orange, he found the huge oil source at Billiton island, Indonesia, where they established the company known now as Billiton. Tuyll's son was Reginald, who married Anna Mathilda van Limburg Stirum, and Julia, the future Lady Sheffield, was their daughter. Reginald died in 1903, so he never saw his daughter married. Reginald was always associated with the turf and hunting, and there had been the occasional scrape and frisk in his sporting life, such as when he was arrested along with his friends for breaking the windows of a Methodist chapel at Bicester. But he appears to merely have been present, and not to have actually thrown any missiles. According to some traditions, he was the person behind the creation of P.G. Wodehouse's character of Archie in *The Indiscretions of Archie* (1921).

When Sir Berkeley and Julia married, there was the obligatory ode written for them, this time by a local scribbler, James Hornsby, whose poem *Sir Berkeley Sheffield's Wedding Day* includes a descriptive account of the country seat:

> *This noble estate is rich with iron ore,*
> *Where workmen are employed by many a score;*
> *The woods and field the truth I'll tell,*
> *They are thick with pheasants and other game as well;*
> *And so for that there can be none complain,*
> *But plenty of sport the gentlemen to entertain.*
> *So here's wishing Sir Berkeley Sheffield and his lady fair*
> *In health and happiness at Normanby Hall may long remain …*

Sir Berkeley was a man with enthusiasm. He clearly loved a project and thought that a man should have plenty of hobbies. One of his most abiding interests was in the breeding and showing of Shire horses. The heavy horse as we know it today goes back to the war horse of medieval times, when a knight required a steed that could carry a considerable weight. In fact, the availability of huge and strong horses was so important to warfare by Tudor times in Henry VIII's reign, there was a statute created to suppress the breeding of smaller breeds.

Attitudes changed as warfare changed, of course, so that in later centuries, there were plenty of other varieties of horse in use for military campaigns. But naturally, the Shire horse was essential for ploughing. As Alex Langlands, social historian, explains:

> On the continent, horses had for some time been used in heavy farm work, but in England, farmers seemed to have resisted the move from oxen to horse for that much longer ... it may have been the English passion for good roast beef that kept so many oxen teams in work.

But the heavy horse was to be very much in use until the encroachment of the transport created after the invention of the internal combustion engine; by the 1960s, their use was markedly in decline.

For Sir Berkeley, Shire horses were his pride and joy. Of course, there were other horses as well, for riding and for the usual hunting. The stables, made in the Georgian years, are still the same today, although most of the buildings are used merely for display of old vehicles. One worker who spoke in the oral history project had plenty to say about the pleasures of working with the horses:

> The stables then ... oh they were beautiful; we used to go with my father to take corn and that for the horses. I mean, there used to be lovely horses in there. ... I can still remember them having horses when I was a child ... all the shopping was done with horses, but by the time I'd got to sixteen, they'd gone on to a van.

We have some idea of the danger of working with heavy horses from Ronald Blythe's famous account of the working people of 'Akenfield' (a made-up name) in his book of that name, published in 1969. In the book, he interviewed Fred Mitchell, who recalled an accident that happened in about 1920:

> The horses ran away from me on the farm. It was only two fields away from the house. … It was a terrible accident; it jagged me all to pieces. The horses bolted in the field and ruined me. … I wasn't in the hospital much more than a month. Then they sent me out on stilts.

In the early Edwardian years, the breeding and showing of Shire horses was immensely popular. There were regular Shire horse shows, and the one held in the Royal Agricultural Hall in Islington in 1902, for instance, was reported on and described by *The Times*. In that report reference is made to the English Cart Horse Society, which was the first name of what was later the Shire Horse Society. The report also mentioned the Royal Commission on Horse Breeding. The shows were major attractions and the report makes it clear exactly how and why these wonderful displays were sustained:

> In almost any other country such work would be left to the state, if it were not neglected altogether. In our own land, however, the principle of self-help flourishes so vigorously that in this society we get a fine example of what can be effected by the hearty co-operation of landowners and tenant farmers, untrammelled by any fostering care on the part of the state. Amongst those still living who have filled the office of president are – in addition to His Majesty the King, who is also the patron of the Society – the Earl of Ellesmere, Earl Spencer, Sir Walter Gilbet, Earl Egerton of Tatton … Lord Belper.

In other words, the aristocrats took charge and made sure that the enterprise went on, and Sir Berkeley was in the forefront of that movement to make sure that the heavy horses survived and were celebrated.

If we need statistics to back this up, again, *The Times* provided some in 1904. On the occasion of that year's Shire Horse Show, there were 862 horses entered. A table of entries from the years 1880 to 1904 included such figures as these:

Year	Stallions	Mares and Fillies	Geldings	Total
1888	204	213		417
1904	481	351	30	862

At the beginning of the twentieth century, the Shire Horse Society had 3,200 members, and had published twenty-three volumes of the *Shire Horse Stud Book*. Prizes awarded at the shows had totalled almost £20,000 by 1900. The celebration of the heavy horse was done with gusto across the land. As *The Times* noted in 1902:

> In the last ten years ... there have been given at country shows 230 gold medals ... whilst since 1895, when the scheme of giving silver medals at the smaller country shows was instituted, 845 silver medals have been bestowed.

Arguably, Sir Berkeley's greatest triumph was with Slipton King at the Shire Horse Show in 1910. This dark bay was just three at the time, and again in 1911, it was singled out for special mention in a *Daily Mail* report. But that year, the King won a prize at last, and his success cornered the market in media interest.

The King was always deeply interested in Shire horses, and it is clear from a variety of sources that he corresponded with several experts and enthusiasts on the animals, one of the most notable experts being Keith Chivers, who spent all his life researching and writing about the breed. He wrote regularly for publications on Shire horses, and in the 1980s he was a key personality in an initiative called History with a Future, conceived by the Shire Horse Society. In his research, he often consulted Sir Berkeley, and their correspondence is preserved at the Museum of English Rural Life in Reading.

There is no doubt that Sir Berkeley's involvement with the breeding and showing of Shire horses was in tune with the times. Keith Chivers points out that in the last decades of the nineteenth century, there was a boom in the breeding of these wonderful, tough creatures. The focus of much attention was when a country estate had a home sale, as was the case with the Earl of

Ellesmere and Sir Walter Gilbey. The latter had such a sale in 1885, and no less than 700 guests turned up, 200 of them coming by train. The event included a champagne lunch for the well heeled, and beer and snacks at a booth for the poorer folk.

Sir Berkeley's animals regularly appear in press reports of the shows, and he was keen on the issues related to breeding. Some of these look strange through modern eyes, but they were important then – matters such as the development of hairy legs. But of course, where breeding is taken seriously, and as big business, the details are important.

Another of Sir Berkeley's enthusiasms was the creation of the Hall's own fire engine and staff. There was an engine house in the stable yard, which housed a space for the engine. Adjoining it was a room for the gear and uniforms. The engine was built by Shand Mason, and the outfit began work early in the twentieth century, and operated through to the Second World War. As the location of the Hall and grounds was far away from any urban area except Scunthorpe, it was the only fire service available to cover a considerable area of farmland and small villages.

In August 1915, Mr Atkinson Clark, the estate manager, received a letter from Shand Mason in London, describing what the vehicle and the service would be:

> We should thoroughly overhaul, clean and repair the boiler, engine, horsebox, wheels, carriage etc, throughout, and overhaul the engine and apparatus, that it would be as good as new. ... The boiler would pass the same tests as those we apply to a new engine and we guarantee it to be in perfect working order. ... If you determine to purchase we shall be pleased to show you a test of the engine at our works, or it will undergo a thorough test on delivery at Normanby Park.

Sir Berkeley was buying second-hand, but clearly it was a sound investment when one considers the constant dangers relating to fire that property was open to at that time. The service was very rarely needed; there is just one instance of its employment, and that is recorded in the oral history project undertaken by Scunthorpe Museum. Also, in David Taylor's compilation about Normanby, which includes quotes from this archive, we have:

I remember the men all running down from Normanby village and diving into the building there at the bottom corner of the yard, putting all those heavy navy blue coats on and big brass helmets and dashing off down Thealby Drive.

That was to attend to a fire at a stack at Thealby.

The early years of the twentieth century saw a number of accidents at the Hall, and that comes as no surprise when we reflect that country work entailed handling horses, guns and dangerous working practices, well before any health and safety legislation came along. In 1904, there was a fatal accident when a groom, Edwin Willingham, was kicked by a horse. He was just 21. Another groom, Maurice Preece, told the coroner's court that Edwin went into a box in which a mare had recently foaled. The press report explained:

His attention was called to the deceased's cries and he found him lying on his right side, the mare being right up against him. Deceased said the mare had kicked him in the stomach as he was giving her the mash.

The medical evidence from a local doctor was that the young man had a ruptured spleen. It was a slow death, and a very painful one.

A few years later, a horse caused another serious accident, this time at the gates to the Park. A Mr and Mrs Marshall were driving out to Scunthorpe when the horse did not take the turn, and the couple were thrown out of the carriage. Mr Marshall had severe head wounds, and his wife died as a result of her injuries. Clearly, it was a perilous time to be around horses, as a report notes: 'Mr Marshall had been to visit the Rev F.A. Jarvis, chairman of the Scunthorpe Bench, who was himself a victim of a similar accident last Friday.' It might have been caused by the fact that the carriage was a light trap, and not the usual police four-wheeler.

In 1909, there was an accident involving Sir Berkeley's head woodsman, Edwin Buckler. He had died, and there was a coroner's court. The *Hull Daily Mail* reported:

What caused Edwin Buckler to fall over will forever be wrapt in a mystery, as the two men at the inquest on Saturday afternoon could not enlighten the court. The men with him did not see him slip, neither did a bough break. The distance, too, was only 13 feet, but being a heavy man, it proved severe enough to cause death. He was head gamekeeper for several years, and then left Sir Berkeley's service for a short time, going back eventually as head woodman.

It was a very sad case: the man left a widow and three children, and the press commented that 'all on the estate knew him well.'

Injuries from horses and other causes from the work done on the estate never went away: they were part of life. Much later, in 1928, for instance, at a celebration with Sir Berkeley at the centre of attention, with the band playing *For He's a Jolly Good Fellow*, Sir Reginald, his son, could not be much involved. The explanation was, in the local paper, 'Mr Reginald Sheffield could not dance, having been kicked by a horse in the riding school at Aldershot.'

The family had kept a London house for many years, and summer holidays were often held in Scotland, and so they were certainly not to be seen around Normanby at every time of the year. In the early years of the twentieth century, their London home was at 8 South Audley Street. One servant recalled, in interview, that it was 'a huge house; it was eight storeys high, and down in the basement there were two horses and carts. Wagons could pass in the basement.' This property was owned by the family until 1922. We know from the memoirs of the Earl of Crawford how much the house rental was from this entry in the Earl's journal:

> We have let our London house from the middle of April for the season and the family will migrate to Haigh. Economy is necessary and the moral value of closing our London house is even more useful than the 600 guineas of rent which Sir Berkeley Sheffield will pay us.

This is a corner terraced town house that was developed in the mid-nineteenth century, having been built in 1744. It is described in the Survey of London of 1980:

The Hall seen from the Park. (*The author*)

The Hall in the grounds. (*The author*)

A side door overlooking part of the garden and pond. (*The author*)

The frieze on the wall by the garden. (*The author*)

The ice house in the grounds. (*The author*)

A view of the pet cemetery at the Hall. (*The author*)

A view of the Hall stables with one of the peacocks that greet visitors. (*The author*)

The attractive Regency stable yard. (*The author*)

A real showpiece: the walled garden. (*The author*)

The greenhouse in the walled garden.
(*The author*)

The Normanby boar. (*The author*)

The little station at the Hall. (*The author*)

Part of the model railway at the Hall. (*The author*)

Portrait of young Berkely with
Sarah Purser. (*Wikicommons*)

MURDER BY A POACHER.

The seat of Sir Robert Sheffield, Bart., at Normanby, was the scene of a most cold-blooded murder, early in the morning of Thursday, the 13th inst. The unfortunate victim was Storey Jackson, a watcher, employed in the game preserves at Normanby. The perpetrator of the sanguinary deed was a poacher, who, we regret to say, is yet at large. On the following day an inquest was held on the body of the murdered man before Mr. Marris, coroner, when the following evidence was adduced:—Edward Thompson deposed as follows:—About ten o'clock on Wednesday evening I and the deceased were employed together in watching the game preserves in Normanby Park. About twenty minutes before three o'clock on the morning of Thursday we heard the report of a gun in the direction of the fish-pond in the park, when we immediately went towards the place. A few minutes afterwards we heard a second report of a gun about thirty yards from us, in the fish-pond plantation. The deceased and I then determined the one to go on one side of the plantation, and the other on the other. The deceased went to the east side, and immediately afterwards called to me " Come this way, my lad," and I went to him. The deceased said to me " they are here." We then determined to jump over the paling into the fish-pond plantation, and whilst we were getting over the pales, a person in the plantation said " keep back or I will shoot you." On getting over the paling, and while attempting to jump over a grip in the plantation, my foot slipped, and I fell short; the deceased sprang further, and got over, when the person in the plantation said " stand back," and again repeated his former threat, at the same moment firing at the deceased, who fell to the ground, gave a groan, and expired instantly. While raising myself up from my knee, after I had slipped, I was knocked down by a blow over the head with the barrel of the gun which had been discharged. On raising myself again, I heard the person jump from the paling of the plantation, and the morning being dark, I saw no more of him. I am quite certain there was but one person. I have no knowledge of his voice, and it was so dark that I was unable to distinguish his person. Neither the deceased nor I had any fire-arms; we each had a stick only. I found a hen pheasant not far from the spot, and I have no doubt that the unknown person who shot the deceased was a poacher.—Isaac Chafer, who had been called out of bed by the former witness, proved that he and some other assistants went to the plantation, and found the body of Jackson, who was quite dead.—Mr. Des Forges, of Burton-upon-Stather, surgeon and apothecary, described the nature of the wounds received by the deceased. The left jaw bone was fractured, and the integuments torn ; the shot had entered the upper part of the chest, passing through the upper lobe of the right lung, and terminating at the back bone; two of the de-

A report of the murder at the Hall, 1838. (*Author's collection*)

What the Hall would have been like during its phase as a military hospital in the Great War. (*Author's collection*)

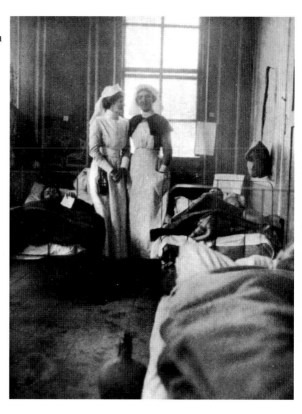

BRIGG BY-ELECTION 1907

A group picture with Sir Berkely, 1907. (*Lincolnshire Life*)

Sir Berkeley promoted in the press. (*Sheffield Evening Telegraph*)

A catalogue advertisement for Fletcher's, the agricultural machinery makers. (*Author's collection*)

Stamped Edition, 6ᵈ.

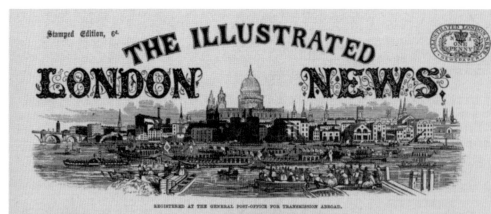

THE ILLUSTRATED LONDON NEWS.

REGISTERED AT THE GENERAL POST-OFFICE FOR TRANSMISSION ABROAD.

No. 1551.—VOL. LV.   SATURDAY, AUGUST 7, 1869.   WITH A SUPPLEMENT, FIVEPENCE

CONSTITUTIONAL REFORMS IN FRANCE.

A Senatus-Consultum has been submitted to the French Senate as the first step towards carrying into effect the concessions announced by the Emperor a short time since. It embraces all the points mentioned in the letter of Napoleon to the Legislative Body. So far as can be judged from the contents of the document, it sustains his good faith to his subjects. How far the Senate may narrow the ground which it is their business legally and technically to define, and which has been granted by the Sovereign in conformity with his interpretation of his people's desire that the political institutions of France might be made to rest upon a broader basis, remains to be seen. Public opinion in France has, to a certain extent, been troubled with doubts, in consequence of the abrupt prorogation of the Corps Législatif, and of the appointment of M. Rouher, subsequently to his resignation of ministerial office, to the Presidency of the Senate. It is likely enough that he will employ the vast influence which his new position gives him in circumscribing, as far as he is permitted to do so, the legal range of the Emperor's concessions. It is, however, manifestly impossible for him, acting, as he must, on the programme furnished him by the Senatus-Consultum, and taking every step, as he will have to do, in the presence of a people jealous of their liberties, to detract very largely from the value of the boon recently promised them in so solemn a manner. Substantially, we apprehend, France will get what the Emperor declared his willingness to give her.

It would be puerile to contend that the concessions to which the Senate is invited to give shape include all that is

AGRICULTURAL MEETING, LINCOLN: JUDGING FOXHOUNDS.—SEE NEXT PAGE.

One of those who drove the amalgamation of the two societies together was Henry Chaplin MP, MFH. It should then be no surprise to learn that there was a foxhound show at this meeting. Thirteen packs made entries and twelve attended. Lord Doneraile and Mr. G. Lane - Fox acted as judges. This illustration shows some of the winning hounds. This show of foxhounds was not repeated though hounds parade annually at the county show.

An agricultural show, 1869. (*The Illustrated London News*)

On of Sir Berkely's Shire horses. (*Lincolnshire Archives*)

RALLY AND FÊTE

In Glorious Surroundings at

NORMANBY PARK
(by kind permission of Lt.-Col. & Mrs. E. C. R. Sheffield)
NR. SCUNTHORPE

WHIT MONDAY - 1954

ADMISSION—BY THIS PROGRAMME Price **1/-**, —or Pay at the Gate **1/6**
Children 6d.   (on the day).

The programme for one of the many events held at the Hall. (*Author's collection*)

One of the experimental tanks at Burton-upon-Stather – an amphibious tank used in trials conducted by the Water Assault Unit. The concrete slipway was specially constructed for the trial. (*The Tank Museum*)

Lady Grosvenor's caravans. (*Lincolnshire Archives*)

Two caravans of the Lincolnshire type. (*Author's collection*)

John Robinson, a former gardener at the Hall. (*John Robinson*)

Joey – the Park's most famous deer until his death in 1979. (*John Robinson*)

there, with an office on the first floor. Scotland wrote about his role: 'My first job was to travel about selecting suitable sites for POW cages where interrogation could be carried out. Then came a series of trips to the various HQs to instruct their personnel.'

So it appears that just along the street, as the Sheffields were enjoying their parties, motor trips and jaunts to the racecourses, there was interrogation of prisoners going on. What the nature of that interrogation was remains a mystery, but one could hardly ask for a more ironical juxtaposition, and the Normanby family were in the very centre of that wartime extreme initiative.

As is shown on television now in some episodes of *Downton Abbey*, the trip to London by a county family entailed a massive logistic operation, with servants and luggage in tow. The servants would stay down in the basement, but the chauffeur and family had their own flat. Another servant recalled how the servants would spend their free time, referring to some time in Hyde Park or shopping in Selfridge's, but there was more:

We'd have our tea in a Lyon's Corner House for a shilling, I think it would be … then on to a play or pictures. Now you're saying, how could we afford that on twenty-eight pounds a year? But you see, we didn't have any food to pay for, we only had our clothes and pleasure, and things were cheap.

This raises the question of the relationship of the servants to the family, other than in the official, hierarchical one. Since there were first household servants in the Saxon world, there had been a structure of importance and status according to social standing. When the eighteenth century saw the solidification of that country house-based aristocratic hierarchy, it came from the proliferation of servants. In the great houses, packed with purchases from the Grand Tour of Europe and designed and landscaped by such luminaries as Capability Brown and Humphrey Repton, the need for more servants had grown as there were more and more specific roles to be undertaken in all areas of work, from kitchen to boudoir, and stables to nursery.

Social historians have pinpointed the 1880s through to the 1920s as the period of decline in this respect, with county families gradually reducing the number of servants. But there is no doubt that the relationship between family members and servants was not always strict and severe; after all, they often went on holidays together, and people have to speak and intermix. In the case of Normanby, the summer journey to holiday in Scotland was illustrative of this. Everyone travelled in a specially contracted excursion train from Doncaster up to Mallaig, which was on the West Highland Line. Of course, staff and family would have been in separate coaches, but there had to be so much activity and time spent together that relationships were bound to develop. For example, as with Lord Grantham on television, Sir Berkeley employed his former army batman in the House.

Sir Berkeley also entered politics. As well as being a family man, with a succession of children, from Robert Arthur in 1905 to John in 1913, Berkeley was always spending leisure time with others, such as his sister, who became Lady Arthur Grosvenor. In between, he went into politics, being elected Member of Parliament for Brigg 1907–10 and again from 1922–29. He was the Unionist MP for Brigg in his first spell in the House, and then he stood as a Conservative in 1922. One of the most well-known photographs of this time is of him with Lady Sheffield and their family, with the caption, 'The man and the family North Lindsey delights to honour.' He stands with one hand resting on his wife's shoulder, while she holds the smallest child. Her face looks rather grim and determined, while Sir Berkeley smiles. The children express a sense of not liking the formal wear and the need to behave.

Before his first term of office Sir Berkeley had been ill. In December 1902, a short press announcement read:

> From enquiries made at Normanby this afternoon, we learn that Sir Berkeley Sheffield is going on as well as can be expected, and that his recovery is only a matter of time, good news of his progress having been received this morning.

He was ill again in early 1908, as the *Hull Daily Mail* reported when covering a political garden party at the Hall:

> Sir Berkeley seems greatly improved in health, and has become quite stout about the face. He was in excellent spirits – as well he might be – and is as determined as ever to be no mere delegate but to speak

and vote as he sees fit on the measures submitted. His explanation of his attitude on the old age pensions should be remembered by local politicians, for satisfactory as it was, his action in going to the lobby along with Mr Cox will be raked up against him in the next election.

There was concern for his health through the years, and later, in February 1927, one press report stated that he was suffering from gout, influenza and erysipelas (a skin infection); but then, should one ever believe press reports? On one occasion, a short piece in a local paper announced that Sir Berkeley was under so much pressure that he was going to sell up everything and leave, to lead the life of a recluse.

In these years before the Great War, the Edwardian age was one of sport, fashionable leisure and all kinds of public display and celebration, and at the time, Normanby Hall was always in the forefront of such matters. Surely nothing is so evocative of that period and of the aristocracy in relaxed mood as the Agricultural and Horticultural Show. Such was the occasion in July 1909, when that local affair was, in the words of one reporter, 'of gigantic proportions'. The same writer noted that back in 1884, the Reverend F.A. Jarvis had started such an event with 'a modest little effort in the vicarage garden', but that in 1909 things were different:

> No one dreamt at that time that the show would grow ... and that it would be looked upon as the great attraction of the summer in North Lincolnshire, but so it has. The removal of the Show to Sir Berkeley Sheffield's Normanby Park set the seal on its success, and the interest taken in it by Sir Berkeley and Lady Sheffield has further added to its effectiveness. ... Sir Berkeley, in a short chat to the *Mail* and *The Times*, said he was glad to get back to Normanby after his parliamentary duties; creeping back home to bed from the House in the early hours of the morning, with the milk, did not agree with him.

At the election of 1910, he did not stand again. In a report in *The Lincolnshire Echo* in February that year, it was stated that at a meeting at the Constitutional Club at Barton-on-Humber, Harry Wilson, chairman of the Conservative Association, said that he had had a letter from Sir Berkeley explaining his reasons for withdrawing. This was after his defeat in which he stood against Sir Alfred Gelder for Brigg. Shortly before that, during the press campaigns, the *Sheffield Daily Telegraph* had backed him, running a feature, with portraits of Sir Berkeley at Brigg and J.R. Starkey at Newark.

A list of proposers and seconders for him was printed at the time of his first spell in Parliament, and this totals 160 names, with the added note:

> and others, making a total of 106 papers handed in in favour of Sir Berkeley Sheffield. It may be pointed out that each paper contained ten names, and they comprised every section of the electorate, from the highest to the most humble, and even included one exclusively SIGNED BY OLD AGED PENSIONERS ... VOTE FOR SHEFFIELD!

In his first term of office, he was involved in debates, as he is frequently mentioned in Hansard reports. Obviously, as a chairman of the bench in the Lincolnshire magistracy, and as a sheriff for the county at one time, his opinions on crime were listened to, and he was always giving opinions in the House on these topics. In May 1907, the subject of a rather testy interchange between Sir Berkeley and John Roche, the MP for Galway East, was crime, as there had been 'outrages' in Athenry, close to Galway city. Sir Berkeley asked Augustine Birrell, who was then Chief Secretary to the Lord Lieutenant of Ireland:

> whether he has received police reports upon the occurrences of 13 March in the neighbourhood of Athenry when shots were fired into the house of a man named Tierney and stones thrown into the dwelling of Mrs Raftery ... whether the first named was injured by this assault and whether these persons are now protected from a repetition of such attacks?

Mr Roche didn't like that series of questions being given to him, and responded with the metaphorical punch concerning crime on Sir Berkeley's own domain: 'Is the Right Hon. gentleman aware that more crime is committed in the Brigg Parliamentary Division than in any four counties in Ireland?' He followed this up the next day with some figures:

1,218 crimes and 14,200 offences in Lincolnshire in 1905 were committed in the Brigg Division of that county ... how many appear under the heading of serious crime; and if he will say how he proposes to deal with the condition of the Brigg Division.

It was as if Sir Berkeley was expected to be in the position of a modern crime commissioner, such was the demand for information. It is clear, though, that he took a wider interest in matters relating to crime. In one case, he was obviously very much concerned with the famous Edalji case. George Edalji was a law student, the son of the vicar of Great Wyrley in Staffordshire. The family were Parsee, an Indian ethnic group whose view of life follows that of Zoroastro, originally an Iranian in the early medieval period. The racial factor is important, because in the first phase of this case, the family were subjected to xenophobic hatred and torment, but this was nothing compared to the consequences of an outbreak of horse maiming in the area, because George was suspected and blamed, then arrested, for the crimes.

There had been a series of anonymous letters, and George was linked to these, his trial and conviction at Stafford following on, with a sentence of seven years of penal servitude. Conan Doyle read the reports and saw the enormity of this. He wrote:

It was late in 1906 that I chanced to pick up an obscure paper called *The Umpire* and caught a statement of the case ... as I read, the unmistakeable accent of truth forced itself on my attention and I realized that I was in the presence of an appalling tragedy.

From today's viewpoint, Edalji's trial reads like an instance of the local police being so determined to prove the guilt of their subject that they shifted the alleged circumstances of offences to suit their prosecution rationale. Conan Doyle saw all this, and he also saw what any perceptive investigator or defence counsel would have seized on immediately: that Edalji had very poor eyesight, and in order to have perpetrated these horrendous mutilations, he would have had to deal with, as Conan Doyle put it, 'the full breadth of the London and North Western Railway, an expanse of rails, wires and other obstacles and hedges to be forced on either side'. Conan Doyle's articles had the effect of a committee being created to enquire into the case, and eventually Conan Doyle's work brought to light a man who was the author of the letters and who, as Conan Doyle put it, 'belonged in an asylum.'

The committee were not convinced by new arguments and evidence; again, Conan Doyle determined to have the man released. What had to be proved was that a certain Peter Hudson was the main author of the abusive letters, and Conan Doyle (with his allies) did what was necessary – they called in Europe's acknowledged expert on handwriting, Dr Lindsay Johnson, who showed that Hudson, not Edalji, was the culprit. Edalji was released, after three years in prison.

In the course of the investigations, there was a clamour in Parliament for the materials of the case to be seen by MPs. In mid-June 1907, F.E. Smith (the great barrister, later Lord Birkenhead) asked the Home Secretary to have a return printed containing all the anonymous letters received by the police in that case, with incidents connected and dates of receipts. It seems that the whole House wanted to play detective. Sir Berkeley added,:

> At the same time, may I ask the Secretary of State for the Home Department whether all the information and documents which were before the Edalji Committee will be made available to Members of the House before the Home Office vote is taken?

He also wanted the 'fullest newspaper report' to be made available. Gladstone (son of the great Liberal) replied that he could not make these provisions. There was great sympathy for George Edalji; Viscount Castlereagh summed this up, asking the Prime Minister if his attention had been called to the fact that Edalji, who was the victim of an unsatisfactory conviction, had lost all his professional prospects. Gladstone remained silent.

Sir Berkeley was also vociferous in relation to the Royal Navy and to such matters as the creation of the Dreadnought battleships and the furnishing of the Home Fleet. It was a time in which the German Baltic Fleet was burgeoning, and the periodicals were packed with features on both the British and the German fleets, the technology of naval warfare, and on strategies for defence measures. Sir Berkeley asked several questions on these matters in his first spell in Parliament. But perhaps one little footnote in a question in

March 1907 gives us the most acute insight into Sir Berkeley's character. This was with regard to a 'Juvenile Woman Suffragette', and he asked the Home Secretary if his attention had been called to 'the remarks made by the magistrate with reference to the case of a girl of tender age who had been brought to London from Lancashire by the suffragettes, and if so, what action he proposes to take.'

In his second term of office Sir Berkely was again prominent in a number of debates, notably in the subject of the payment of MPs. This had been introduced in Lloyd George's days, with the 1911 Parliament Act. Sir Berkeley, in a speech made in Brigg in 1922, made it clear that he opposed the payments, arguing that taxing the public for the support of people who might not really represent their views was not desirable. He was implying that politics being pragmatic, views and actions could change, and one's MP may well act in opposition to the promises made at election. Well, that has always been the state of things in power games, one might argue. But Sir Berkeley had many strong views on political life, including what he considered to be the disaster of a government with a large majority and a weak opposition.

Chapter 4

The Locality and the Great War

There never was a good war, or a bad peace.
Letter to Quincy, by Benjamin Franklin

In the years shortly before the Great War there had been widespread militarism. Aristocrats, with money and leisure, were often mixing with writers, politicians and artists who had interests in guns, horses and travel. Between the Anglo–Boer War (which ended in 1902) and 1914, these quasi-military outfits flourished. An influential one that recruited Sir Berkeley was known as the Legion of Frontiersmen. In 1904, a letter to the papers called for men of adventure and experience to gather together as a special force of fighters, and auxiliaries to be a resource for Britain in emergencies. The appeal was for women as well as men. The guiding spirit was Roger Pocock, a man who had fought in the Boer Wars and had also been in the ranks of the Canadian Mounted Police.

Pocock had proved himself to be a suitable leader for such an intrepid band, having accomplished such feats as riding unarmed from Canada to Mexico to grasp the world record for long-distance horse riding. He had also been to Russia, so again, he appealed to Harry as a kindred spirit. He saw the need for men of his own calibre as a national reserve. This came at a time when there was an atmosphere of 'spy fever' in the land, as it was known that Germany was developing as a nation with a massive and threatening military status. It is impossible to criticize Pocock for any lack of commitment: he was constantly active and engaged in matters military. In fact, his Legion, as *The Times* explained on Pocock's death, had an interesting inception:

The first meeting took place in his bedroom, and it was decided that members must have had either war training or have done some form of frontier work. The original idea was that the Legion should be 'the eyes of a blind Empire'.

A typical member was the writer William Le Queux, who responded and joined the ranks, along with other men of action such as English writers Morley Roberts, Edgar Wallace, and a number of war correspondents. Behind all this was the sense of failure after the huge loss of life fighting the Boers, where ability as sharpshooters and snipers had shocked and rocked the British Army. Now here was a bunch of shooting men and hardy explorers who were gathering to form an unofficial reserve army. It was a sign of the times.

In April 1906, *The Times* reported on the organization, and gave this staggering information:

We are informed by the secretary of the Legion of Frontiersmen that the formation of the corps which is to be a civilian and self-supporting force, has long been approved by the Secretary of State for War and that 6,000 men with colonial, frontier and sea experience have applied for enrolment.

It appears from this that the media thought that the Legion was more than a case of 'boys' toys' and dressing up for parades.

All kinds of celebrities showed a great interest, including Sir Arthur Conan Doyle, who wrote a long letter to *The Times* with a cunning plan of his own relating to the Legion and its potential uses. He suggested that:

A thousand motorists, the number of which I am sure could be trebled or quadrupled, should organize themselves on the first news of invasion, could instantly fill up their cars with picked riflemen ... and convey them, with a week's food ... to the danger points.

He then appealed: 'I should be much obliged if every motorist who reads of this scheme and approves of it would send a card to that effect to the secretary, League of Frontiersmen, 6, Adam Street, Adelphi.'

The list of dignitaries who were members is impressive. A typical instance is that of the actor Sir John Martin Harvey, who was made a lieutenant of the Frontiersmen for services to recruiting in the Great War. The same applies to Sir Berkeley and many others. The explorer and writer Harry de Windt, for example, was also engaged in recruiting work in the first year of the war.

There was also the colourful character Sir Claude Champion de Crespigny, who sounds like a man about to joust; in fact, he was an adventurer, soldier, and also, in his writing capacity, war correspondent of the sporting paper *The Pink 'Un*. Sir Berkeley was in interesting company, to say the least.

In January 1907, the Legion engaged in a colourful piece of promotional activity: they gave an assault-at-arms in Manchester on the evening of the 20th of that month. A reporter noted that 'an interesting feature of the programme were two despatch rides – one from Newcastle-on-Tyne and the other from Portsmouth.' We have no information regarding Berkeley's involvement in this.

By 1909, matters concerning the Legion were a little shaky, as the press reported that a patriotic fund was to be started by *The Times* in order to save the apparently failing organization of patriots. It was reported that Pocock had made a desperate appeal 'to get sums of money from a shilling upwards.' But this was a strange rumour, as the piece was followed by a statement that the Legion was in a 'flourishing condition'.

Sir Berkeley relished the meetings and brotherhood activities of the Legion, and it gave him the chance to open up his social circle. The records of the family expenditure in the first three decades of the twentieth century reflect this widening cultural life, and we will return to this topic in chapter 7. There were other members in the area, but it is difficult to track down any definite organization such as a sub-branch; for instance, Vivian Hollowday, who was to be distinguished by acts of bravery in the Second World War, such as reported in *The London Gazette* for 21 January 1941. He was born in Barton-on-Humber, and in 1916 became a member of the Royal Society of St George, and was also a member of the Legion of Frontiersmen. He was distinguished by 'two acts of gallantry' – rescuing airmen from burning planes. He died in 1977.

Another footnote on the subject comes from Richard Askwith in his book *The Lost Village* (2008), in which he writes:

Spent an afternoon in Scartho [Grimsby] with a part-time bus driver who claimed to be a colonel in the 104-year-old private army called the Legion of Frontiersmen, whose *raison d'être* seems to be to protect the British state in times of crisis using outdoor skills more commonly associated with the Scouts. . . . His force was down to three men, two of whom were 'not in the best of health'.

This humour and ridicule is not uncommon in writing on the Legion. It is unjustified, as there was far more to it than adult Boy Scouts activities. But certainly it appears to have been active around North Lincolnshire in Sir Berkeley's lifetime.

On the eve of war, the press reported, succinctly, that 'Sir B. Sheffield's Offer Accepted', after he had offered his services during the current crisis. The *Morning Post* wrote: 'Before he entered the bonds of matrimony, Sir Berkeley was in the diplomatic service. Normanby Hall is to be turned into a hospital if needed.' There was a tradition of Sheffields doing diplomatic work. Back in 1878, at the time of the crisis between Russia and Turkey, Lord Lyons went to try to help create a peaceful settlement, and with him went Sir Robert's brother Frank, Berkeley's uncle, as private secretary. He had been in the office of secretary in the Paris Embassy since 1867.

Sir Berkeley played a part in recruitment, along with his peers. One of the real ironies of this was pointed out by Chris Bailey and Steve Bramley in their book on the 1/5 Battalion, Lincolnshire Regiment, that it was a short while after a recruitment meeting held by Sir Berkeley in September 1914 that a local man, Lance Corporal William Selby (from Scunthorpe), was killed. He was with three other men from D Company when a shell hit the trench. The authors quote a note by Captain Dixon:

While patrolling our front last night we came into contact with enemy patrol: four of the enemy were wounded and brought into our lines while two more were killed. Three men of our patrol were wounded. Stretcher bearers Presgrave and Dunderdale, at great personal risk, under heavy shellfire, came out and recovered three wounded.

It must have been deeply upsetting for the Sheffields to read of such losses. Sir Berkeley, as virtually every person of standing had done across the land, had given the obligatory patriotic speech. In 1914 he spoke to Scunthorpe recruits. *The Lincolnshire Star* recorded the event:

Recruiting in Scunthorpe is progressing favourably and Corporal Broadhead … and that energetic civilian Mr G.H. Plows enlisted fifty on Wednesday. They could have probably doubled that number but fifty only were required that day and these have joined the 5th Lincolns (Territorials). The men paraded at the Drill Hall at 7.45 and before they marched to the station Sir Berkeley Sheffield addressed them.

Sir Berkeley told the men that he would not wish them goodbye, but 'god speed', and added that they were going to join the most honourable career any man could join. *The Lincolnshire Star* continued:

The cause was a just one and the fight would be a fight to the finish. Of all things they must be most careful of their health. They should drink as little alcohol as possible, smoke few cigarettes and keep to the good old-fashioned pipe. When they felt inclined to curse he asked them not to curse their hard luck or hard work, but if they had to curse anything, curse the blooming Germans (laughter and applause).

The Scunthorpe men marched away to war to the accompaniment of a band playing *The Lincolnshire Poacher*. We have to wonder whether the recruits listened to their local aristocrat; they must have been fully aware that he would be smoking and drinking later that day, and perhaps cursing also, not caring much for his health.

Together with virtually every other country house in 1914, Normanby Hall adjusted to extreme needs and pitched into the war effort by converting itself into a civilian hospital and recovery centre. In all the shires of the land, the aristocrats and the new rich with roomy houses and plenty of land began the adaptation into some kind of medical work. In towns and cities with hospitals and universities, this was an ideal opportunity to maximize their facilities and use their expertise in all the people skills attached to hospital care. But in the country, although of course there was always a local medical man, often the county families themselves adapted and learned new skills.

There was also the home front challenge of helping and treating the vast number of wounded servicemen who were invalided out of the war. Eventually, more than 3,000 stately homes across Britain were to be used as military hospitals. At Brocklesby Park, where the Chums of the Lincolnshire Regiment had started their training, medical staff were installed. Photos survive showing the nursing staff in the makeshift 'wards'. It opened as a Voluntary Aid Detachment hospital in March 1915, and by February 1919, it had treated 570 wounded men. Among those admitted were two soldiers from the Cleethorpes Zeppelin raid.

In addition to this work, the Sheffields also gave their South Audley Street home in London to wartime medical work. This was a link to M. Mouravieff-Apostoi, a diplomat who had served in a number of places, including Madrid, Lisbon and Athens. He switched to Red Cross work, being the delegate for the Russian branch. With his wife, he established a hospital at the Sheffield's London home. One press comment on this indicates their sheer determination and resolve:

> This hospital was managed and maintained by them until they were ruined by the Revolution in Russia. Friends, and a concert at the Queen's Hall, enabled them to carry on their work for the British wounded until March 1919.

One of the photos from Brocklesby at the time shows Marica Pelham, Countess of Yarborough, who worked as the commandant. The eldest son of the Countess and Lord Yarborough, Charles, Lord Worsley, was killed in action at just 27 years old, so they had good reason to do more than their share of tending to the masses of young men who had come close to death at the front. Normanby followed suit, and a general approach was adopted in respect of converting these spacious family homes into makeshift hospitals or convalescent establishments.

Across North Lincolnshire and Yorkshire there were several similar country houses doing the same work, and men from the Greater Grimsby area, as well as men from Yorkshire, turned up as far away as at Normanby Hall and at Frickley Hall, in South Yorkshire. Staff kept autograph and commonplace books, and one such volume has maxims and homely philosophy from servicemen, reflecting the mood of the time, such as this from a nurse, in January 1916:

The truest greatness lies in being kind;
The truest wisdom in a happy mind.

Or this, from Private P. Cartwright of the 5th KOYLI:

Here's health to the Kaiser.
The Crown Prince as well.
I wish all Germans were in Germany
And Germany was in … (well, you know)

Within a week of the declaration of war, *The Times* announced: 'The Duke of Sutherland's organization for the registration and equipment of country houses and convalescent homes for wounded soldiers and sailors has been amalgamated with the Incorporated Soldiers' and Sailors' Help Society in order to avoid overlapping.' A committee was formed, and by 13 August 1914, they had received 250 replies to the Duke of Sutherland's appeal for houses to be in the scheme.

Naturally, there would have to be training to back up these measures, and classes in emergency first aid and nursing were set up in a number of places. Sir John Collie, for instance, at the University of London, began courses, along with the London County Council. The whole production machine swung into operation, down to the introduction of every grade of nursing uniform, made by Debenham and Freebody. A typical transmutation was this:

Princess Henry of Battenberg has been lent No. 80, Hill Street, Berkeley Square, by Jeanne Lady Coate, and has placed it at the disposal of the Army Medical Service as a hospital for the reception of wounded officers.… It will be known as Princess Henry of Battenberg's Hospital.

At Normanby, the Hall was used as a Voluntary Aid Detachment hospital. The VAD initiative was universal, and allowed for the most numerous recruitment of medical staff from the general civilian population. The experiences of these nurses has been very well recorded in archives and memoirs, and in publications produced during and after the war there were extensive writings on the training. One of the principal professionals involved in such training was Mrs St Clair Stobart, who founded the Women's Convoy Corps, which ventured into Eastern Europe. She wrote a spirited defence of the amateur nurse:

> The experiences I have gained in the Balkans have taught me many things. As a result I am convinced that if women are to become efficient members of a National Service and are to be allowed to give to the nation's defences of their very best, they must no longer be played with.... They must be trained and adopted by the Territorial Army. Women must no longer be regarded as apocryphal numbers, but as worthy to be included in the inspired text of the national religion of Patriotism.

Mrs Stobart, and others like her, were listened to; not only did the women come forward for training, but in many cases, the lady of the house played a prominent role, and this happened at Normanby. One girl working there at this time had this memory, recorded by the oral history archive:

> It was a hospital when I went for the soldiers. They all came from Sheffield you see and they used to come backwards and forwards. Some of them were quite ill when they came, and some of them were recuperating. ... There was a matron there and lots of VAD nurses, and Lady Sheffield was the commandant. She wore a different uniform to the others. They just kept one wing for themselves, Sir Berkeley's study was turned into a dining room, and that's really the only room they had downstairs. The soldiers had all the downstairs.

There was accommodation for around sixty patients in the Hall; along with the volunteer nurses there was a professional sister. Included amongst the amateur nurses was Clara Spilman, whose niece wrote a biography of Harold Dudley, who had come from Sheffield as a young man to work in Scunthorpe and who became one of its most prominent citizens, mainly in the arts. Clara's niece's biography includes this memory of concerts being given at the Hall in the war:

Every few weeks my father took a concert party over from Scunthorpe to entertain the soldiers and those who were caring for them. My mother remembered the great kindness of Sir Berkeley and Lady Sheffield, Mrs Wills (Lady Sheffield's sister) and Canon Jarvis, the vicar of Burton, all of whom welcomed the artistes on many occasions. The concerts were much appreciated by patients and nurses alike and many of those who had sung in the Apollo Choir, the Choral Society and the Operatic Society gave generously of their services. Percy Holt, Gerald Holder, May Markham and Jack Bickerton were some of the many artistes my mother recalled who regularly sang bright and cheerful songs, some of them from Gilbert and Sullivan operas, and there were humorous items from Tom Young, the blind comedian from Frodingham.

There is no doubt that the recovering servicemen were given all the leisure time entertainment that could be mustered. Across the country, these country hall hospitals were only too keen to provide what the popular culture of the time relished: fancy dress balls, sketches and concerts. The same author notes that her mother 'recalled a fancy dress ball when, dressed as "Cherry Ripe", she was able to guide the faltering steps of soldiers who were on the road to recovery.'

Sources tend to agree that 1,248 wounded servicemen were catered for at the Hall, and these were men from Australasia as well as from British regiments.

There was also the contribution that could be made because of Sir Berkeley's Shire horse expertise. When war broke out, there was of course a huge demand for horses for use in the war in France and Belgium. As is now widely known from the book *War Horse* by Michael Morpurgo, the death toll for the horses serving was incredibly high. The requisition and purchase of horses by the War Office was rapidly undertaken. As Keith Chivers puts it: 'All over the kingdom, motley collections of horses were assembled for inspection for military buyers, who worked so fast that in twelve days they had acquired 140,000 animals.' Anyone owning horses was likely to find that they were defined as a 'compulsory vendor'. Siegfried Sassoon, in his war memoirs, wrote of his favourite mount being requisitioned, and he wrote in his account of the trench war that he saw the horse later, at the front, and his emotional attachment to the animal was profound.

No doubt Sir Berkeley had similar experiences, but he was involved in the collection of horses for service. As Keith Chivers points out, if it wasn't because of the stud books and breeding programmes undertaken several decades before the war, there would have been problems:

> If the civilized nations had decided upon such a war as this in 1880, instead of 1914, they could not have achieved it – they had enough men available for slaughter. But could not have supplied the horses. We do know the hard work of the stud book societies had at all costs to be continued. They had been bred for peace, and their horses were being used for war.

By the end of 1916, there was a register compiled by the director of remounts, which had been sending horses to work with the Belgians and with others. At that time the list had 797,174 horses.

Particularly interesting with regard to the use of cavalry in the war is recent thinking about tactics. Whereas in the past there has been much criticism of the use of cavalry – this being seen as an anachronism in a war with such reliance on new weaponry – now there have been reassessments that actually see sense in the strategy of having massive cavalry forces ready for a 'sweep' after a bombardment. Such was the plan at the Somme in 1916, but of course, the German trenches there were so well dug in and solid that the expected easy victory of the infantry never happened.

Sir Berkeley was involved in the war in yet another capacity: he was a diplomat, and he accompanied Alfred, Lord Milner, to Russia on the mission that sailed from Oban on 20 January 1917. Milner was a member of the War Cabinet in 1916, appointed as Minister without Portfolio in the Cabinet of five men. He had vast experience in administration, principally in South Africa, during the Anglo–Boer War of 1899–1902.

Between the party's arrival in late January, and their return to Scapa Flow on 22 February, the mission's objectives had been frustrated. They were there to discuss the possibility of Britain supplying Russia with armaments to back their push from the East against the German/Austro-Hungarian forces on the Eastern Front. From the moment of the party's arrival in Port Romanov, close to Murmansk, Milner and his aides, including Sir Berkeley, saw the chaos in front of them, and the lack of any proper management. Munitions lay around the docks, unsupervised, and there was no apparent order in the place. They moved on to meet the Tsar and other dignitaries at Tsarskoe Selo, where the Tsar and his family were living at their beloved Alexander Palace. But this became a succession of dinners and lunches. Along with Milner and Sir Berkeley was the old soldier, Sir Henry Wilson, whose was later murdered by the Irish nationalists, and he could see that the mission was wasting its time. He wrote home, 'Milner tells me that yesterday the Emperor and Empress made it quite clear that they would not tolerate any discussion of Russian internal politics.'

We now know, of course, that the Russian Revolution was but weeks away. There is a group photograph of the delegation and their Russian hosts at one of the main halls of the palace. This conveys powerfully the atmosphere of pointless dressing up and posing that went on, instead of actual war policy discussion. More meetings were undertaken, this time in Petrograd; it became clear to Milner that Russia was so disorganized that it had not co-ordinated and gathered its own resources for weaponry and support materials of military offensive. He noted the inadequacy and the feeling that the mission had no chance of success.

Naturally, this failure was not something that the government wanted the public to know; hence, *The Times* reported on the return of the mission and their report was in keeping with the empty rhetoric that tends to proliferate in such circumstances:

Further, in response to assurances from the representatives of the greatest Russian city that no efforts were being spared in order to bring the war to a victorious conclusion, Lord Milner, speaking of the results already achieved by the Petrograd Conference, said that he had no doubt that everything was being done in Russia ... to enable their armies to vanquish the foe.

We know from Milner's own diary that his deeper thinking about Russia played little part in this mission. For instance, he wrote this insight:

I began to understand what was meant by the menace of the Russian Bear. I thought of Madame Novikoff's words, 'The Germans have reached their day, the English their midday, the French their afternoon, the Italians their evening, the Spanish their night; but the Slavs stand on the threshold of the morning.'

As for Lloyd George, he knew that, after Milner's party reported on the true state of Russia, that an opportunity had been missed. He wrote in his diary about the waste of armaments and the poor organization:

> These circumstances ought not to have been a surprise to anyone who knew Czarist Russia. In fact, it was always a subject of gossip and jest whenever Russian needs were discussed. But the Allies ought to have made a common effort to grapple with these conditions years ago.

As for Sir Berkeley's part in this, we have to read between the lines, and also we need to consider just what he was involved in that still remains a shadowy phase of his life. For instance, he was involved in diplomatic work as early as 1897, when he was attaché to Paris; then, in the Great War, he also had a post in the Foreign Office and was a member of the Supreme War Council. The latter was another of Lloyd George's creations, being established after the Rapallo Conference in November 1917, with the aim of considering the possibilities for settlement in the event of an armistice. So, Sir Berkeley was a part of all this, and he must have travelled in France from time to time in between other commitments. One of these commitments was as a steward of the Jockey Club, and no account of Sir Berkeley would be complete without a mention of his penchant for horse racing. Even during the war, he was busy with this, having started out in the sport in partnership with Sir Samuel Scott, MP for Marylebone West and later Baron Farquhar. Scott financed the *Evening Times*, which was essential reading for racing enthusiasts, and it was with that paper that Edgar Wallace had his first big break, being racing editor.

Sir Berkeley's horses featured prominently in the racing calendar, and he moved among the movers and shakers of the turf. When he took the office in the Jockey Club, it was 1921, and he had perhaps a little more spare time.

Of course, Scunthorpe being renowned for iron and steel production through its history, there had to be some kind of impact on the Sheffield family and estate from that industry. Back in 1859, Charles Winn, who had gained some land after enclosure, was in a shooting party. Reg and Peter Cooke, historians of Scunthorpe steel, describe what happened on that day when the shooters went out for some fun:

> One of the party picked up a clinker and said that he thought it was ironstone. Mr Winn sent for George Dawes and John Rosebury, who visited the site and confirmed the presence of ironstone. The beginning of heavy industry had arrived.

The Sheffields had a close connection with the Winns. Harriet Dumaresq, the sister of Priscilla, the wife of the second Sir Robert, married Rowland Winn, the First Baron Oswald. He was a key player in the growth of the Scunthorpe area as an industrial epicentre of the country. His family were from Appleby Hall, just a few miles away from the Hall. Rowland was MP for North Lincolnshire from 1868 to 1885, and he was behind the massive building project that produced almost 200 new houses in Frodingham, Scunthorpe. The Frodingham ironworks had arrived in the first years of the century and the workers needed housing. When he became Baron St Oswald he settled at Nostell Priory, in Yorkshire.

The discovery of ironstone was to lead to major industry, of course, and also to the communication channels related to that production.

A few years after the war, Sir Berkeley was also involved in the development of more housing in Scunthorpe. In 1923, a war memorial known as the Crosby Angel was made and placed by the school in Crosby (a part of Scunthorpe). Sir Berkeley financed houses and a school for that area, helping the effort towards regeneration and renewal after the terrible loss of life the Great War brought with it.

Chapter 5

Estate Workers and Servants

Honest labour bears a lovely face.
Patient Grissill, by Thomas Dekker

In the nineteenth century, when the country estates were thriving, being bought and developed by the 'new blood' of the masters of industry as well as by the likes of the first Sir Robert Sheffield, there was an overarching vision of paternalistic rule and order. The British Empire was being maintained at great cost, and the focal power that sustained it was with the profits from production and from the aristocratic base. The latter meant that the network of old landed families worked by way of a microcosmic mirroring of the larger, cosmopolitan picture. In other words, the country estates had their hierarchy of owners, families and workers, and their smaller but often self-sufficient communities were part of that broader, macro-economic structure.

The wealthy upper middle classes provided the administrators and managers in this society, and the aristocracy supplied, until the last years of the century, most important of all, employment. The country houses employed vast numbers of servants and estate workers. There were speciality jobs in all trades; some of the key members of the house staff, such as the gamekeeper, would be expected to have an entire panoply of skills and expertise. But in many cases, the workers had a special responsibility, and that had its integral skills.

The point is that there were lots of staff, up until the social and occupational changes at the *fin de siècle* and then the Great War. The latter, of course, brought about a revolution in terms of the aspirations of working people, offering them 'careers' and new modes of work. For women, who had proved their new identities as workers with far more to offer than changing bed sheets or making dinner, the post-1914 world was to bring radical new opportunities as the vote came to them (the process completed in 1928) and as education opened up more professions.

But from the first Sir Robert's time in 1818 to end of the century, the demand for servants and estate workers was massive and consistently sustained by a thriving community – in a sense, a concept with its own powerful domain, nurtured by its own families and their resources and labour. The modern reader studies the explanations of the servant job description and stratification with awe. On the website Countryhousereader (see bibliography), for instance, the point is made very cogently. Even if we restrict the listings to female servants, we have this for the top of the tree, the housekeeper:

> The housekeeper was the undisputed head of the female staff. Such a role demanded a huge array of responsibility and the best character was dependable, sensible, prudent and honest. Known as 'Mrs' regardless of marital status, a good housekeeper was probably a terrifying woman to work with if you were young and inexperienced.

Between her and the lowliest – the scullery maid – there were at least seven other servants: cook, head nurse or nanny, housemaid, kitchen or cook maid, laundry maid, nursemaid and dairymaid. Even this bare list omits other minor roles such as the storeroom or stillroom maid.

In the twentieth century, the general national pattern in this respect was to change markedly, but Normanby Hall was an exception to the trend. The building of the new servants' wing in the first years of the twentieth century suggests undoubtedly that there were plenty of servants to cater for. One former worker gave a very detailed account of the quarters in the oral history project:

> As you went into the servants' hall, immediately on the right and left were the staircases to the first and second floors. Immediately on the left on the ground floor was the kitchen. ... Then you went up a second flight ... big stone stairs. At the top ... was the butler's pantry where all the silverware was kept. ... Coming back on the other side was the housekeeper's apartments, then you had this long servants' hall.

At that time (about 1910), there were fifteen domestic staff, from butler to 'odd man' – the general handyman and spare assistant who was, in football terms, the utility player in the team. The butler was obviously a key member of the whole house management; he was married, and had a house in Normanby. The butler's province was supervision and maintenance of plate, food and drink, linen and taking control of the serving at dinners. Clearly, he would be memorable, and indeed, one oral history reflection recalls a typical scene of a butler's presence:

> The butler used to sit at one end of the table and the housekeeper at the other. The butler served the meat and the housekeeper served the vegetables. The men sat down one side of the table, and the girls the other.

A useful way to ascertain the importance of the Hall as local employer in this context is to look at the county directories, as they list occupations for towns and villages. Normanby village was not listed separately, but Burton-upon-Stather was, and in *White's Directory* for 1856, we have John Champion, saddler, James Coulthurst, gamekeeper, amongst the farmers and tradesmen. But thirty years later, in the directory, we have an interesting group of Hall employees listed, including: Henry Allen, head gardener; Alexander Ansell, schoolmaster at Normanby; John Birnie, steward, agent and head woodman to Sir Robert; Richard Heightley, gardener; Nicholas Preston, wheelwright; George Wilkinson, wheelwright; James Wood, blacksmith; and John Wood, blacksmith. Significantly, the list also includes George Tosh, 'civil engineer and ironmaster (North Lincolnshire Iron Co., Frodingham)'.

Finally, with servants and Hall workers in mind, if we then look at the equivalent entry for a 1933 directory, we find in Burton some new occupations, such as Ernest Dain, cashier to Sir Berkeley. We also have 'Normanby Estate office' listed, and a sub-agent to Sir Berkeley, one Edward Ponsonby, and Dan Stanworth, the Park's forester. As noted earlier, there were the fifteen house servants, and clearly, through the century between the first and last of these directories, the notable developments in the nature of the work in the Hall and Park were in more specialized jobs, and in the villages around the Hall, there had been new categories of workers.

Historian Lucy Lethbridge has given a detailed account of the changes in domestic service and in service in country estates in her book *Servants*, in which she comments on the changes during the inter-war years:

> The 1930s may have seen the final flowering of the great house but it bloomed with a spectacular show of traditional colour in those final years. ... Vast, labyrinthine holding areas of tradition and ritualistic routine continued to function as if the social changes of the inter-war years were remote.

As to the workers outside in the fresh air of the Park and the woods, attention must turn to a very important person in the enterprise: the gamekeeper. We know a little about the early gamekeepers, at the end of the eighteenth century, because their names were recorded when certificates were issued in the process of controlling the game duty. In September 1790, for instance, the press listed 'persons to whom certificates have been issued by the Clerk of the Peace for the parts of Lindsey in the county of Lincoln'. These included William Richard Wilson, of Normanby Hall. Along with the names came the 'manors' in which they could act. The information included in these returns gave the people 'by whom deputed', so that, for instance, a few miles down the road at Amcotts by the Trent, a certain Samuel Belton, a grazier, had a certificate, deputed by Wharton Amcotts Esq, and he was restricted to that place.

In 1862, near the end of the second Sir Robert's regime, the keeper was James Coulthurst, who had been in the job since 1850. But by the early twentieth century, the name of Matthew Grass appears on the records, and that surname is arguably the most celebrated in English social history. He was one of a dynasty whose keepers stretched across the land. The Hall story has already embraced the criminal chronicle of violent encounters between keepers and poachers, but with the twentieth century, there was far more involvement in the work.

David S.D. Jones, social historian, has told the story of the Grass family, and written widely on their lives and work. Being gunmen, of course, some went off to fight in the Great War, while others at home played a part in forming Local Defence Volunteers. Jones points out that 'Some Grass gamekeepers were deliberately kept out of the armed services by keen shooting men.' Five of the Grass family died in the Great War; Jones notes that when the war began, 'gamekeepers rushed to join the armed forces.' After the war, as cuts began to hurt in high places, some of these men lost their positions. But at Normanby, Matthew was still employed as gamekeeper. There were casualties in their ranks, of course, and in a feature article by Mr Jones, one of his pictures shows two keepers wearing the distinctive outfit of injured servicemen, such as would have been staying at the Hall.

Mr Jones has pointed out that, at the time that Matthew was at Normanby, his brother Frederick worked at Belvoir Castle as head keeper, and his cousins Frederick and Henry were at Eaton Hall and Lambton Castle respectively. It was a very impressive record for the Grass 'dynasty' of keepers. Matthew died in 1954. He had been in charge from 1904 to 1954, and so is one of the key figures in Normanby history. He had been born in 1871, on another famous country estate – Belvoir Castle. He did what all the men in his profession did: absorbed the skills and ways of working from father at first, and then after a switch to work across the land in Cheshire, he had some time with his Uncle John.

Midway between the villages of Burton and Flixborough was where a small place called Burton Wood House was established, and that was Matthew's home. As with everyone who worked as a gamekeeper, he had a range of responsibilities, and his expertise covered work with dogs, horses and the animals always kept in smallholdings. His appearance may be gleaned from some extant photos: one shows him in about 1930, gun in hand and wearing leggings, boots, jacket and soft hat. In a group snap, he is shown with some beaters at a shoot, and he stands in the centre of the group, with his dog at his feet. Most interesting of all, one could argue, is a wonderful shot taken in the 1920s, showing him on a cart, with an older man at the reins. Matthew looks almost dapper – with a shirt and tie, flat cap and pipe in his mouth. He is perhaps on his way to some event.

The keeper's life was circumscribed: it was dependent on the cycle of the seasons and the concomitant events and chores. Obviously, a central phase of this was the partridge season, and by the last days of October, the Sheffields were usually back home from their summer holidays near Loch Morar, and they would be back for the pheasant shoot. As David Taylor notes in his oral history compilation *I Remember Normanby*, there was an interesting cluster of guests, and sometimes there was royalty in their number. Of course, the pheasant shoot had to be a success, and for that to be so there had to be enough birds. Through the centuries, that responsibility fell to the gamekeeper, who had to collect eggs and make sure that young birds were born and raised. The chicks had to be fostered and well fed, and so the keeper was on guard duty as well as being a supervisor watching the whole process.

There is no doubt that the Sheffield possessions needed a team of keepers at most stages in the history of their lands, especially if we bear in mind that their domain covered Burton and six other villages.

The keeper is, of course, inextricably mixed in with the culture of shooting and the shooting parties provided for house guests and local friends of the family. One memory from the oral history project gives a glimpse of the mid-twentieth-century scene:

> There'd be an awful lot of activity in that stable yard. There'd be extra cars in, suddenly come in, they'd just park in the yard. And then there was a big horse-drawn covered wagon, for bringing game back in. There'd be quite big parties sometimes; we're talking of groups of twenty-five, thirty people trudging off for a day's shoot.

In the 1970s, the photographer Martin Parr took some marvellously evocative images of a shoot in Yorkshire, showing the beaters, some shooters and close-ups of gun dogs. He captured the spirit of the shoot: the long day would have lunch *al fresco* included, and the keeper and beaters would be given refreshment as well. The dead birds were gathered and carried to a store in the Hall yard. This was perhaps Matthew's biggest day of his working year, and he made it happen.

David Jones, the expert on the Grass gamekeepers, explains what would be happening on days when there was no shooting: 'The keepers spent many hours shooting, trapping or laying strychnine baits to kill rats, squirrels, stoats, magpies, hawks and other vermin.' Mr Jones points out that each keeper put out a display of the beasts he had killed, and back in the day, he would receive some cash for each verminous creature. It might come as a shock to the modern reader to learn that such creatures as magpies and squirrels were defined as vermin.

There are also memories from local families, such as the Elwes family of Elsham Hall, a few miles from Brigg. In their biography of the singer Gervase Elwes, Winefrida and Roland Elwes have this memory:

> I remember one shoot at Normanby where our neighbour, Sir Berkeley Sheffield, always showed excellent sport. It was a very grand party with the old Duke of Cambridge as the principal guest and a great number of others. The Duke was beginning to fail and often missed, and so Gervase was put behind him. The effect of the Duke's shots was to make the birds fly very high, and the large crowd of country folk, who had assembled to watch royalty shooting, were full of loud exclamations of admiration as one towering bird after another fell to Gervase's gun.

The inter-war years had brought great changes in all areas of life. Specifically for country estates, some facts and figures say a great deal. For instance, Lindsay Duguid, writing on the decline and fall of the country houses at the time, wrote, 'In 1913, a quarter of peers owned two or more country houses: between 1918 and 1930, 180 houses were destroyed, thirty by fire in 1926 alone.' But for many there were still opportunities for pleasure as well as for expansion into new areas of life, and the Sheffields fell into that category. A look at Sir Berkeley's accounts reflects the family lifestyle in great detail. He was undoubtedly continuing his expenditure on a grand scale, as he had done since the early years of the century, when earnings from ironstone began to escalate. The figures in the accounts show a constant succession of investments, loans, payments from loans, cultural adventures, and, of course, the obligatory material possessions of an aristocratic life, from expensive cars to school fees.

The basic underlying fact, when it comes to the twentieth-century Sheffield story, is the income from ironstone. When that substantial income was acquired – showing, for instance, a net profit in the estate accounts for 1903 of £14,624 4s 6d – there was a lifestyle to achieve and maintain. Today, we need to multiply that figure by about fifty to see the spending power there.

In the early years of the century, the major project was the new building: the servants' quarters. But on top of that we have, for instance, expenditure on agricultural works, payments to family, insurance policies, payments to local builders and tradesmen, and such items as Sir Berkely's subscription to the Marlborough Club. A gentleman of his status had to have a London club, along with the London house, and all the accoutrements that gather on top of these. Income came in steadily from royalties, the money from Conesby alone averaging around £350. The accounts reflect the values and aspirations too. It has to be recalled that living up to the high culture required, with all its commitments and style, was an immense strain on resources. Anne de Courcy describes this kind of life in her biography of the Curzon sisters, and it is close to what the Sheffield situation would have been:

> The grandeur, the sports, the pleasures, the elaborate clothes washed, ironed, mended and packed by the lady's maid or valet, the dressing gongs, the carriages, the silver tea-things on a white lace cloth beneath a cedar tree on the lawn, were expressions of a society secure in its own power – which extended over roughly a quarter of the world.

A man in Sir Berkeley's situation was expected to throw parties and be a presence in the social round of the 'seasons'. There were such matters as horses and schooling for the children, and private tutors were obligatory. 'Finishing' in Paris, or somewhere equally esteemed in Europe, was essential. All this brought protocol and the demands of 'the done thing', too. Again, Anne de Courcy gives a typical example:

> That season [1922] saw the return of the full-scale evening court for the first time since before the war. A ruling from Buckingham Palace stated that the trains of gowns were to be no more than 2 yards long instead of 3 so that they would train at most 18 inches along the ground.

At Normanby Hall, the lifestyle also meant charitable work as well, and that had to be financed, such as payments made to the Needy Widows Clothing Fund in 1903, or to the Queen Victoria Clergy Fund. There were any number of subscriptions through the years to local and county organizations too, such as the Brigg Fatstock Society. But on the whole, in the years before the Great War, there was a very pleasing and substantial progress, in spite of the changes in the economy at the highest level after the Liberal reforms.

After the war, there were great changes. Life for the Sheffield family was now very much more a London enterprise. The children were growing up, and education took centre stage. The Normanby Estate Company was going well, with H.G. Atkinson-Clark in charge of the estate office at Crosby, and all kinds of local schemes and projects underway. Dividends from various shares came in, and there had also been investments in war bonds. From 1920, the accounts show a gradual escalation of costs that came along with new enterprises and expenses; 1920, for instance, was a very full and busy year. As well as allowances paid to family members and private charity work, there was the cost of stepping into modernity and its technology. For instance, one entry is: 'Insurance – Lady Sheffield's car', and another, 'Lady Sheffield's Buick car repair', which cost £7 10s. There were several cars around, and even a motorbike and sidecar.

Cars and racehorses figure prominently in the costs of the family's lifestyle, and Sir Berkeley, being an enthusiast for the turf, owned horses and invested in a Newmarket stud. Other footnotes to life's costs included a payment to an investigator named Percy Groom. But basically, there is nothing very different or astounding in the financial records of the time. All the aristocrats with homes to run obviously had massive expenses; keeping a London house in Kensington was, in itself, a full-time occupation. Everything was linked to cachet – to how one was seen. Oscar Wilde's joke in *The Importance of Being Earnest* is pretty close to the real attitudes:

Lady Bracknell: You have a town house, I hope? A girl with a simple, unspoiled nature, like Gwendoline, could hardly be expected to reside in the country.

Jack: Well, I own a house in Belgrave Square, but it is let by the year to Lady Bloxham. Of course, I can get it back whenever I like at six month's notice.

Lady Bracknell: Lady Bloxham? I don't know her.

Jack: Oh she goes about very little.

Lady Bracknell: What number Belgrave Square?

Jack: 149.

Lady Bracknell: (shaking her head) Ah, the unfashionable side.

As well as the comment about the snobbery of an actual London location, there is the question of income – the renting. Sir Berkeley had rents too, and that was entirely typical of the time. People with money invested, and they did so across a wide spectrum so that there was always a multiplicity of financial transactions, in and out, to a succession of places. One determining factor in all this was the arrival of super tax. When Lloyd George originally introduced this, it was at 4 per cent on incomes of over £200k, but when the war came, the rate steadily rose. Income was best being active, kept in transactions and in a variety of places where it would earn.

There were unfortunate footnotes to the chronicle of staff and their lives and work. In the 1920s, there were two particularly tragic losses in this respect. The first concerns a gardener called Robert Thistlewhite, who was found dead at the Hall on 1 August 1922. There was a coroner's inquest as it was a suspicious and unexplained death, and the resulting story was sad indeed. The quiet man was estranged from his wife, who was living in Harrogate. This wife, Edith, came to identify her husband's body. One press comment carries so much unspoken meaning: 'Owing to her husband's drinking habits, she obtained a judicial separation three years ago and had only seen him twice since.'

Ernest Allen, another gardener at the Hall, told the court that Robert had lived in the bothy. Not long before his death, he and some other workers had received notice of their termination of employment, and it appears that Robert had asked for time to go to Scunthorpe 'to put his name on the books.' The main summing up of his character was:

He never complained, was always cheerful and quite happy. He never said anything about his domestic affairs, and the witness [Ernest Allen] never asked him about them. If anyone told the witness the deceased had taken his own life, he would be very much surprised.

But that was in fact the case. The medical witness asserted that the poor man had taken weed killer, which contained arsenic. Another gardener, Frank Hornsby, found the body. He said, 'I gave him a slight push with my feet ... and told him it was time to get up.' He assumed that Robert had taken too much drink the night before. The police gave a clear account of what had happened:

> Sergeant Battram said the deceased had apparently been sitting on his bed vomiting and he looked as if he had slipped to the floor. In his possession, witness found a 10s note, 1s 6d in silver, five coppers, watch and chain and other articles including a cheque book on a Harrogate bank.

The coroner noted that a combination of domestic and financial worries had been a determining factor in the case. The verdict returned was 'suicide while temporarily insane'.

A few years later, Eileen Victoria Hamilton-Cox, the private secretary to Lady Sheffield, was killed in a riding accident. Eileen, accompanied by a groom, was out at West Halton top when her horse bolted. As horse and rider galloped in the Winterton direction, Eileen was thrown and suffered a heavy fall. She was taken to the War Memorial Hospital in Scunthorpe, but did not recover, so severe were her head injuries.

Eileen was only thirty-nine, and was involved in local charity, being secretary to the Normanby Park District Nursing Association and the Normanby Women's Unionist Association. The local press commented that she was a 'popular personality' who was 'well known throughout the whole of North Lincolnshire'.

Of course, as well as the staff, there was a large circle of professional friends and acquaintances around the family and the Hall. It is not an easy task to find and describe most of these people, as they range from vets to engineers and mechanics to seed merchants. Only occasionally do we have glimpses of these people, as in the case of Dr James Couldrey, whose obituary in 1912 notes that he was a formidable presence in Scunthorpe, where, as well as being Sir Berkeley's doctor, he was Medical Officer and Public Vaccinator for the area, as well as surgeon at the Frodingham Cottage Hospital and an author on medical matters, published in distinguished journals such as *The Lancet*.

Memories of working at the Hall in the post-war years have been recorded, at least in accounts of conversations and oral history work, but one former worker, John Robinson, kindly allowed me to use an extract from his autobiography, and in this passage he recalls beginning work as a gardener at the Hall. He had already had some experience working for the local Parks Department and then had a spell in the army. Here he recalls the beginning of his time with the Sheffields:

I was working one day at the school and suddenly the Parks Superintendent's van pulled up and out he strode towards me across the main football pitch that I was marking out. He always seemed to rush everywhere.

'Now then, lad' (he always called me lad), 'there's a new job coming up at Normanby Hall.'

Now, Normanby Hall was the big stately house where the Sheffield family lived who owned most of the land where the ironstone ore was mined for the steelworks. To cover death duty problems, they gave it to the Scunthorpe Borough Council, whose intention was to open it up to the public as a furnished house and with over 300 acres of gardens, grounds and deer park in which to roam.

They had appointed a head gardener to start on re-instating the place as the grounds especially had fallen into a rather unsightly state.

The parks boss went on: 'The trouble is, though lad, there's a house in the village that goes with the job and you will need to be married – have a think about it then lad.'

I replied almost without thinking: 'I'll get married then.'

Who was the more surprised of the two of us, I am not sure, but here I was, about to embark on another one of life's great adventures.

Jean and I had indeed talked about getting married but were waiting a while until financial circumstances picked up a little. I had now been approached by the Park's boss with this offer of the under gardener's job at Normanby Park, with a house provided. It was an opportunity not to be missed, I thought, assuming Jean would be happy with it. In hindsight, there would be problems in future life that we did not fully consider. That would all be due to always having a job with a tied house. It would be many years later that those problems would rear up and bite us! However, all those years back we were over the moon with the opportunities on offer, and a decision was needed rather quickly.

He was married and started work at the Hall, so he gives us a vivid account of what the place was like just after the Council took over:

It was a great house, in the village – semi detached and with a large, long garden. It was a mere 300 yards from my workplace. Although the grounds of the Hall had been somewhat neglected, the remnants of the old, once elaborate Victorian country house garden was still there, with greenhouses, sunken beds, walled gardens, lakes and the like. The new head gardener I was to be under, Jack, was a fine man: fair, knowledgeable and good to work for. We enjoyed each other's company and his wife was pleasant and her and Jean got on well together. He had come from a private garden up north, where his boss was the head of some big insurance company. One of his boss's daily orders was to be provided with greenhouse nettles all the year around, which he would plunge into every day in order (he thought) to be cured of his rheumatism, and other aches and pains. Jack always said it was a big change – from growing them to spraying them.

Jack had a passion for rhododendrons, meconopsis, primulas and the like. These are all plants that love acid conditions and the Park soils were perfect. We set about renovating the walled garden, streams, bogs pools, woodland, stone walls and all. And it was really interesting and rewarding work. I had moved up in the world and had a small DMW trials motorcycle, which was useful for getting around the Park. Jean was still working at the steelworks' typing pool about 5 miles away, and managed to get a lift to work each day with a man in the village, or if not, there was a handy local bus service. Things were going well at work and I enjoyed the large garden in the village with the vegetable plot, and the space to grow my favourites such as dahlias. The people in the village were really pleasant, and made us welcome, and we soon had many friends, including the men I worked with, who also lived locally. My natural history interest was still there and intensified with the new species and varied habitats around the iron ore mines and semi-heathlands of the area. My photography improved along with that and I used it as a means of recording the many new discoveries I made.

The old iron ore mines and the edge of the Park were wonderful sites for wildlife, with heathy areas, small pools, wet areas, stony quarries and woodland. There was a superb kestrels' nest in a massive old oak tree and to photograph it would need scaffolding – and lots of it! This is where my friend, Ken, who worked as a builder for the local council, saved the day!

Over a period of two weeks, we managed to get the scaffold tower up to nest height and then got the hide on the top platform. It was about 50 feet high. At that time, all my photography was on monochrome film, which is unfortunate as I secured some good pictures of the adults with their chicks. These would have been a real bonus in colour. I did use my black and white negatives for lectures though, as I had mastered the art of making them into slides that could be projected. There were whinchats, too, nesting in the heathy, brackeny areas, and these were quite a rarity in the county – even more so these days. This was the first species I used colour transparency film on, and the results were quite good, considering my equipment. I was still using the homemade telephoto set-up. What made the images even better, was the fact that the male bird came back to the nest carrying a small heath butterfly for the chicks. This picture was a milestone for me as it was the first picture I ever had published in a large magazine. It made a full page in the *Encyclopaedia of Birds*. I was pleased with that.

Chapter 6

The Hall in the Second World War

He is an Englishman
For he himself said it,
And it's greatly to his credit
That he is an Englishman.

                     HMS Pinafore, by W.S. Gilbert

In the years immediately before the Second World War broke out, life for the Sheffield family and their workers and servants was very much what it had been since the beginning of the century, with the addition of the unavoidable presence of the Lysaght iron and steel works not far down the road towards Scunthorpe. This was officially the Normanby Park Works, run by John Lysaght, which had opened in 1911. At first it had three blast furnaces, and during the Great War it had supplied steel to the great manufacturers for the production of the Dreadnought tank. In Lincoln, only 25 miles to the south, the powerful company of Foster and Co was producing the Dreadnought, and the city had been in the first rank of tank development and innovation for some years before that.

In the 1930s, the Normanby Park Works was intensively developed, with a new state of the art coke oven battery and new steel furnaces. Then, in 1937, there was a sinter plant built. As war approached, it was hard to avoid the fact that the Hall and Park were nudging up close to these giant industrial bases, and of course, when the air war was imminent by 1939, the military minds would turn some attention to the fact that Scunthorpe might be a major Luftwaffe target. As it turned out, the town escaped the worst of that horrific regime of terror.

In 1936, Sir Berkeley became the first Charter Mayor of Scunthorpe. He had, one might say, a finger in every pie when it came to local matters. If we have to isolate one of his many philanthropic and practical schemes and engagements in this regard, it might be the Normanby Park District Nursing Association. This had been affiliated to the Queen Victoria Jubilee Institute for Nurses, and the accounts for it running in 1931, for instance, show the contributions made to it from the Hall. They received a £5 donation from the Normanby Estates Office, and another £3 10s for the rent of a garage. Again, those figures need to be multiplied by fifty for a rough equivalent in 2016. It is hard to underestimate the value of that organization through that period of thirty years from its beginnings to the accounts issued in 1931, as those years saw several terrible outbreaks of influenza, to say nothing of the care of the war wounded. It provides one instance, from hundreds, in which the influence of the hall was seen.

In a memoir of life in Burton-upon-Stather, Winn Readhead has given us a rare insight into the time when the army arrived. Winn wrote:

> At first there were no restrictions to the tented camp and we roamed freely through it, entering tents and talking to the men. They had funny accents and we thought at first that they were Americans but later learned that they were French-Canadians.

Winn also had memories of the period before the military arrived, and what was done in preparation:

> Lorry loads of slag were needed to reinforce the old footpath and the stile was removed. ... Lowe's farm billeted some of the invaders, as did the Ferry House Inn, and a shed was built on the green as a barracks for others.

The Second World War was in full swing, and Normanby was once more about to be an important element in housing and adapting to troops. What was happening was part of a truly momentous event in British and European history: preparations for the Normandy landings. But even well before that, in June 1940, Royal Artillery anti-aircraft units were in the area. In the period of intense bombing by the Luftwaffe, naturally, Scunthorpe, being an important industrial centre, was a key target, and so ack-ack batteries were deployed around the area. Fortunately for Scunthorpe and Normanby, there was very little Luftwaffe assault; there was simply one comparatively minor incident at Flixborough on 12 May 1940, when the nitrogen works was hit and five men were killed and others injured.

It was Hull that really felt the full power of the bombing, and of course, being just across the Humber, the city's suffering was seen by people on the South Bank, evident in the red skies after incendiaries had been dropped.

But it was in 1944 when the Canadians and others arrived, with the purpose of training regarding preparation for D-Day. The infantry had to have somewhere to practise that was similar to the actual landing places envisaged in France. In addition, though, there was the detachment from the Specialized Armour Detachment Establishment, who had to train in preparation for their crossing of the river Rhine. These were part of the 79th Armoured Division, which had been formed in 1942. They were very nearly scrapped, but thanks to the foresight of Sir Alan Brooke, they were saved, and Major General Sir Percy Hobart took charge. His detachment was to become known as Hobart's Funnies, because they were working with experimental tanks, created specifically for functions in water.

These vehicles were to be seen on the Trent; some of them worked by crossing the river with the use of an invention known as a pendulum, which was shot across to the opposite bank by a rocket, followed by a winching operation to move the tank across.

There were all kinds of military around Burton, of course. Valerie Mercer's father was there, and she has provided this account of her father and the Hall:

The Royal Artillery had various ack-ack batteries in the area. The soldiers who manned these were billeted at Normanby Hall. The cooking was carried out in the old servants' quarters. The area to the north of the Hall, now a car park, was the parade ground.

Valerie adds that her dad said it would be 'a cushy billet' and had assumed that he would be in the building, not out in a tent. She then gives a full description of the camp in her piece *A Soldier's Tale*, written for the Winteringham Local History website:

So early one morning the residents of Burton-upon-Stather got quite a shock when they heard loud rumbling sounds of traffic going down Stather Hill. There was a continuous column of army vehicles ... the area was immediately cordoned off. The first camp for the soldiers was along the river bank behind a house known as Lowes Farm. ... A barrier was erected across the road where the Ferry House Inn is. The wooden Nissen huts were erected on the green, being the base for the Military Police. My dad would have been on guard at this time, as he was a 'vulnerable points' guard, which means they guarded anything which was top secret.

In 2010, Pete Day of the Burton-upon-Stather Heritage Group wrote about his interview with John Porteous, who had been in the Water Assault Wing at that time. He was actually in the Argyll and Sutherland Highlanders, but was drafted in to work as a shallow water diver. Pete Day wrote, referring to John Porteous:

The aim, in his words, was 'forward thinking' – all in preparation for crossing the Rhine, as the river Trent, at that point, was similar in current, speed, tide etc. The Tank Ramp at Burton-upon-Stather was constructed by the Royal Engineers, almost all of the materials ... sourced locally.

John Porteous also told Pete Day about his work as a diver, including this experience:

Attached to the lines at low water he had to make his way through the mud with instruments attached to his diving suit, the centre of the river being iron stone made for easier 'walking'. Another idea was the rolling out of canvas covered in coconut matting from an apparatus attached to the front of the tank. There was a reel at the front of the tank which unrolled the matting. This, John says, was 'a winner', enabling the tank weighing some 50 tons fully loaded to go over the mud without sinking.

In the war, notably, the Division saw action at the battle of the Scheldt estuary, which has been labelled Operation Infatuate, and also at the Roer Triangle (Operation Blackcock), as well as at the famous Rhine and Elbe crossings. Normanby and Burton can be proud that they played a major role in the development of Hobart's Funnies and consequently in the battles that helped to win the war in its final phase.

At the end of the war came the 1945 General Election, with a Labour victory. This was a real sign of change at the most widespread level; although the general history of that event is well documented, there are not too many personal accounts from the time in the Normanby area. Fortunately, Janet Rothery wrote an account of the events of that election with a sound knowledge of the locality. She came from a Labour family and recalls meeting the successful candidate, Tom Williamson. It was the end of the line for the Sheffields and their political ventures, and June Rothery reminds her readers that in the Brigg constituency, formed in 1885, there had been a steady dialogue between the parties. Of course, all this was happening after the widening of the suffrage, first in 1918, when all men over 21 had the vote, and then in 1928, when the same applied to women. Janet wrote of the importance of that Labour victory and she also recalled a vivid image from the post-war election campaigning:

> I think on one trip to Dragonby on the Hill, a row of houses on the edge of the Scunthorpe iron workings, my father got eight voters including children into his army truck. There were two seats at the front and the back had no seats, as soldiers had sat on the floor inside, facing each other with their kitbags.

Tom Williamson won with a majority of 8,000. Then, in the by-election of 1948, Janet's mother was the agent for the new Labour man, Lance Mallalieu. Janet rightly includes in her memoir an account of the tied cottages in Normanby, and it is difficult to avoid the political perspective when she writes:

> When my mother canvassed in Normanby, the estate village ... she had many a whispered conversation with the people living in the tied

cottages. They told her that they wouldn't dare to vote for any party but the 'squire's' as they might be evicted. ... She promised them that she would keep an eye on the box and make sure it was a secret ballot.

The Hall is not seen in a good light at all if Janet's memoir is to be believed, as she adds this account of her mother going to take some Labour leaflets to the Hall:

When she climbed the steps to the front door she rang the bell as she could find no letterbox, or so the story goes. The butler opened the door and, seeing her red rosette, brushed her roughly backwards, saying, we do not want your filthy stuff here. She fell over on the steps and laddered her lisle stockings, and scraped her shins to bleeding point. He had already slammed the door shut.

Clearly, everything was not all wine and roses; the village may have been developed with some kind of idyllic vision, but the rich and poor oppositions of British history were being challenged, and there was the Hall, on the edge of the growing industrial town of Scunthorpe, with its strong Labour presence, beginning to feel the fallout from massive social and economic change. The war had played its part in intensifying all that increasingly visible disparity of wealth and status that had always divided the land. It was the challenge to paternalism that was really becoming a tangible force in the still expanding town and its satellite villages.

Sir Berkeley died in London, after a short illness, on 26 November 1946. *The Times* obituary summarized his diplomatic work and touched on his racing and business interests. Perhaps one of the most interesting insights into Sir Berkeley's nature was in this memory from a housemaid, recorded in the oral history project:

A proper country gentleman. And when I used to be taking the meal, the tray upstairs you see, he used to hear the door go, and he always used to come and meet me and take the tray off me, when I had to take the tray up to the boudoir you see ... and if he heard me coming with a log basket he used to come and carry it for me.

Lady Julia Sheffield died on 14 July 1952.

Local writer Edith Spilman Dudley, the wife of Harold, who was mentioned in the chapter on the Great War, was a notable poet and personality around North Lincolnshire, with book titles such as *Lyrics of Lovely Lincolnshire* (1946) and *A Lincolnshire Garland* (1953). She wrote a long biographical profile of Lady Julia for a regional newspaper as an obituary, and in that piece she said far more than the usual complimentary statements about public life. She really brought Lady Sheffield's personality to the fore:

> For the keynote of Lady Sheffield's life was service. She was not just a figurehead but a real leader and worker, as many of us who worked with her can testify. My husband organized many concerts for the patients when, during the First World War, Normanby Hall became a convalescent hospital for our wounded men, and there Lady Sheffield could often be seen, scrubbing tables and sharing all the menial tasks as well as giving devoted and skilful nursing to many grateful servicemen.... She responded generously to all appeals for support, but in addition to public benefactions there were countless deeds of mercy and kindness. ... I recall her constant visits to one old lady – the widow of an estate worker – who was bedridden for many years. The walls of her little cottage were almost covered with photographs of the Sheffield family.

It would be hard to find a clearer example of the quasi-parental attitudes and acts of the landed aristocracy in England. It backs up the kinds of depictions we have had in film and television in which paternal (and in this case, maternal) acts of service were done towards the workers who kept the estates going. Another insight into Lady Sheffield is from Wilfrida and Roland Elwes, mentioned previously, from Elsham Hall:

> I also remember Lady Sheffield, our neighbour ... sitting up all night in a cottage with a child which had whooping cough. The mother was worn out with nursing it, and so her ladyship took a turn, and I believe saved the child's life.

Edith Spilman Dudley gave us a sharp insight into that side of Lady Sheffield's character, but there was also the public side, and Edith points out that 'Lady Sheffield graced every occasion whether as a charming and dignified hostess at county balls when Sir Berkeley was High Sheriff of Lincolnshire, or at hundreds of functions of a simpler character.'

Chapter 7

Social History: the 1920s to the 1960s

The good old rule
Sufficeth them, the simple plan,
That they should take, who have the power,
And they should keep, who can.

Rob Roy's Grave, by William Wordsworth

The social history of the Hall in the late Georgian and Victorian times had been one of survival and then progress as the economic forces were at work everywhere. One of the most notable aspects of the Victorian period for the estates of the nobility was the rise of the new millionaires, mostly from the ranks of the business entrepreneurs of the Industrial Revolution. There had been a gradual assimilation of blue blood and new rich. This had impacted on the wider Normanby family, as Ambrose Phipps, who had been Earl of Mulgrave, and was later the Third Marquess of Normanby, married Grace Foster in 1903. She was the granddaughter of the great Yorkshire industrialist John Foster (who had died in 1879).

However, regarding the Sheffields themselves, their marriages had reflected the equally general trend of keeping the blue blood pure, as it were, taking in the Dutch connection with van Tuyll, and the link to the Portlands when the second daughter of the second Sir Robert became Lady Arthur Grosvenor.

This was the spine of the Sheffield narrative throughout the nineteenth century – growth and conservatism in everything, and this in a world in which money, land and title still guaranteed status and progress. But from the later years of the nineteenth century, massive changes were signalled; from the late 1880s through to the Great War there were about 200 new peers made, and many of these were from the new rich rather than from landed aristocracy. Adding to this, along came the Great War, and the massive social revolution brought about by that meant that from about 1920, things were never going to be the same again – for anyone.

In an 1856 map of Lincolnshire concerning country seats, Denis Mills has shown very interestingly what the situation was with regard to ownership of the seats when Sir Robert was enjoying the heyday of the estate. This shows that the Sheffields were one of just eight titled families in the county, north of Lincoln. The map shows very clearly what the situation was several decades before the really marked increase in the rise of the new rich had an impact.

One is struck by the camaraderie at times of either crisis or of important social occasions; this was sometimes wonderfully enhanced by the 'characters' in the assemblage of biographies we meet along the way in the story of the Hall and Park. One of the most colourful in this category was undoubtedly Lady Arthur Grosvenor, one of Sir Berkeley's sisters. She had married the Duke of Portland, and they had a property along the coast at Healing, near Grimsby: Healing Manor. It was acquired in 1882, and was the country estate for the Portmans. One of the most amazing Lincolnshire tales from the whole of sporting history comes from that manor: the tale of the racehorse, Cure-All.

In 1845, Cure-All was walked from Healing across the land to Liverpool's Aintree racecourse to run in the Grand National. He was a rank outsider. After all, he had been bought at a Horncastle horse fair for a mere £50, after being inspected and noted as being lame. As the Healing Manor website explains:

> On the day of the race the ground was so hard from overnight frost that the start of the race was delayed for several hours and some horses were withdrawn. ... However, as Cure-All was there and facing a long walk home, it was decided to let him run and he surprised the experts by winning the race in a then record time.

Lively and dramatic history was built into the Grosvenor story. Lady Arthur Grosvenor's husband was the second son of the Duke of Westminster. A studio photograph of 1898 shows Lady Grosvenor sitting in a rather strained posture, wrapped in a luxuriously designed dress, with lacy cuffs and epaulettes; one would hardly think that this was the woman who had a passion for the outdoor gypsy life of the lanes and fields. She tended to come to the Hall with attendants and two caravans. One servant recalled:

> I think it would be seven or eight and we were walking along the Thealby Road, then there was this woman coming with a huge dog. . . . She asked us over to her caravan. It was marvellous and she'd another couple with her, they'd a caravan of their own … and she'd a lovely blue frock on right to the ground with silver braid. And this huge dog, it was as big as me. She said, 'It won't hurt you.' Nearly knocked me down.

This was the same Lady Grosvenor who contributed an introduction to a novel called *Napoleon Boswell* by Herbert Malleson. The reviewer for *The Spectator* made it clear that she knew her stuff:

> Lady Arthur Grosvenor in her interesting preface draws a sharp distinction between the real *Romanichel* [the genuine gypsy people] and the so-called gypsy of the present day, the posh-rat (half-breed), 'the common caravan or cart-dwelling vagabond, who has not a drop of Gypsy blood in his veins'. The same writer makes a point of her open-minded attitude to the whole subject: '[she] dwells with enthusiasm on the fine qualities of the old Gypsy families – their reverence for the dead, their genius for companionship, and their instinctive good breeding. All that she says about their picturesqueness may be readily granted.'

In the last decade of the nineteenth century, and in the Edwardian years, there was investment and speculation everywhere; it was the age of expansion in many senses, and the Sheffields were no different to everyone else with money to invest. Life was all about calculated risks as new industries and technologies came along. In Oscar Wilde's play *An Ideal Husband*, performed in 1895, Wilde takes the subject of overseas investment as the basis of the scandal at the heart of the play's moral dilemma. Mrs Cheveley, who is blackmailing Sir Robert Chiltern, says of the Argentine Canal Scheme that it was 'a brilliant, daring speculation'. It was an age of risk, and so it was exciting, and Wilde makes excellent fiction out of it. But for investors such as Sir Berkeley, it was a case of having a number of investments – borrowing, lending and keeping irons in the fire. That is what almost everyone did.

One of the most significant for Sir Berkeley was the advent of the Great Central Railway. He was to have a locomotive named after him, when the Class E was created by John G. Robinson. A sequence of these locomotives were named after the directors of the railway, and in 1913, Sir Berkeley's turn came, with Number 436.

The GCR was opened in 1897, after the Manchester, Sheffield and Lincolnshire line changed its name. The main line of the company ran from Manchester to Cleethorpes. Naturally, the Sheffields would have a keen interest in the railway, as it was crucially important to all the local communication links and industry. Long before this time, the Earl of Yarborough had done the same for the Grimsby area, and the first sight to greet people leaving the train at Grimsby today is the impressive Yarborough hotel.

Sir Berkeley was indeed involved in a major phase of modern social history: the GCR also owned ships, and their cross-channel service became an integral part of the massive migratory movements from Eastern Europe to America. The railway constructed harbours to work in a neat line of integration between sea and land, and from 1863, when all the railway firms were given the go-ahead to organize these cross-channel routes, the business really took off. The GCR became the key element in that lengthy period of emigration stemming from, in many cases, the pogroms and persecution of Jews in Russia under the Tsarist regime. The trains and ships would use Grimsby, and of course, that port was across the North Sea directly from European ports. It was all very smoothly organized, with combined tickets issued to cover the journey. Across the Humber, a similar traffic was in progress, the immigrants coming to Hull, mostly from Scandinavia.

Closer to home was his involvement with the North Lindsey Light Railway. Bryan Longbone, social historian, has explained this development in depth, and he has provided the wider context, such as the growth of light railways in America and in Europe, mainly in agricultural areas. This was related to the dichotomy between the high profits on the major lines (which of course meant more profit) and the marginal profits in light railways.

Bryan Longbone notes that just after the passing of the Light Railways Act of 1896, the Axholme Joint Railway was made. That is not far away from Normanby, and the precept was there. Much earlier, Rowland Winn had proposed the Frodingham and Humber Wharf Railway.

As Bryan Longbone tells the story, Sir Berkeley and Rowland, with their involvement with the Lysaghts Works, saw the need for a railway to transport their iron ore in the local area:

> The initial construction of the NLLR was with a single line, being prior to the agreement of Lysaghts with Sir Berkeley regarding the iron and steel works. At the southern end of the line, much ore mining was ongoing and a pathway had to be found through such. … In other words, the maximum cash return from the land.

Rowland Winn really was an outstanding entrepreneur in his time, which was an era when such men were forcing their way into new wealth in all corners of the land. He lived at Appleby Hall in the mid-century, and he saw the value of railways in the new age, establishing the Trent, Ancholme and Grimsby Railway in 1866. Appleby Hall, as described in *White's Directory* for 1872, was 'a substantial mansion enlarged about the year 1822 … commanding extensive views of the Wolds'. A traveller visiting the place in 1828 noted, 'The Hall is a comfortable house built about 1770–75 and now enlarging for a hunting lodge.' Their line stemmed from the George Winn who, in 1660, was created a baronet by Charles II. Rowland's first success with his ironstone, when he saw the value of his commodity, went back to 1859. He never looked back.

Railways remained in the blood as far as Sir Berkeley was concerned, and later, that meant the model railway that was installed at the Hall. This interest began in 1910, when Sir Berkeley asked for a scale model loco to be made by James Carson and Co. The loco was given the name *The Great Bear*, after the ship commanded by Sir Berkeley's ancestor, Edmund Sheffield, in the combat with the Spanish Armada of 1588.

The Scunthorpe Society of Model Engineers now run the Normanby railway and their website has photos showing the family fun in progress with the model railway, including one picture showing Sir Berkeley aboard, and the engine being driven by his daughter, Diane Mary. Later, *The Great Bear* was to travel away, being with new owners, but as the website of the Scunthorpe Model Engineers relates, there was a happy ending when the loco came home again:

> On 2 June 2006 at 9.30 am, a box was lifted out of a car, opened up, and *The Great Bear* once more could breathe the air of home. … Also the first time any one of us had seen the engine.

Sir Reginald Sheffield was there on that occasion (grandson of Sir Berkeley) and in a few months, the loco was back on the track: 'After some work, on a cold, damp and foggy day, 20 December 2006, *The Great Bear* was again on the track at Normanby.'

After the Great War there were momentous decisions to be made in terms of the area around the burgeoning town of Scunthorpe – tracts of land extending towards Flixborough to the west and towards Crosby, which was later to be part of Scunthorpe – and also the topic of what part the land around neighbouring Brigg would play in any reorganization. This question of amalgamation had arisen as the iron and steel industries grew. The issue affected Sheffield land mainly in respect of the stretch of good land going from the edge of Normanby Road, across the Trent valley to Flixborough.

The census returns show that in the Scunthorpe district, covering the villages of Brumby, Frodingham, Crosby and Ashby, the population had been 7,621 in 1891, 11,232 in 1901, and 19,677 in 1911. In 1918, the population was estimated as being about 28,000. The big question in 1920 was, how should amalgamation take place, and also, following on from that was the subject of the rates for sewerage and water. There was an enquiry held in early October 1918, and E.J. Naldrett acted on behalf of Sir Berkeley, who clearly had an important part to play. The chairman pointed out that there had been no statement from the Hall on the matter, and Naldrett, who had by this time been briefed, summarized Sir Berkeley's view:

> [Sir Berkeley] suggested that the whole of the land to be de-urbanised in Crosby should be adjoined to Flixborough and to this counsel for both proposals also agreed that other de-urbanised districts should be

left until local feeling had been tested as to which parish they wished to become attached – Mr Naldrett referred to Sir Berkeley's land on the west side of the ridge line in Crosby, which Sir Berkeley desired should not be included in the new district. It was purely agricultural and rural land, and no authority had a right to take in land which was essentially rural and which would not become urban in a practicable time.

When Sir Berkeley was made charter mayor, the Charter of Incorporation, presented in 1936, was national news. *The Times* reported:

Scunthorpe has been elevated to municipal status as a result of its remarkable expansion since the district was amalgamated in 1919. With a population of nearly 40,000 inhabitants, the town is now producing something like one tenth of the steel output of the country.… As President of the Association of Municipal Corporations, he welcomed Scunthorpe as the newest borough in England.

The press were eager to point out that Sir Berkeley was the main 'benefactor of the district' and in a more substantial article, *The Times* made a special mention of the steelworks at Lysaghts, and summed up the modernity and status of Scunthorpe: 'Scunthorpe is becoming more and more the administrative centre for the large agricultural area in which it is situated.' Sir Berkeley was a crucially important part of that celebrated progress. But *The Times*, aware of its reputation, could not resist a swipe at the town's lack of classical learning:

The town has been granted a coat of arms with the motto (the Latinity of which may have to be revised) *Refulgit Labores Nostros Coelum* – the heavens reflect our labours – a reference to the nightly glow from the industrial establishments which can be seen for over 30 miles.

Perhaps Sir Berkeley should have brought in one of his more academic chums to check the Latin. It appears that the only error is that the first word should be '*refulget*'.

The mayoral celebrations were not only remembered nationally: local memoirists have marked those celebrations as a special time. Maud Mary Knott, for instance, writing in 1987, recalled:

> In 1936, the town received its Charter of Incorporation when Sir Berkeley Sheffield became Charter Mayor. There was a great celebration held at the Football Field, now known as the Old Showground, home of Scunthorpe United Football Club [no longer so, being replaced by Glanford Park]. I remember taking part in the celebrations as a member of a combined choir, when we sang *Nymphs and Shepherds Come Away*.

As Scunthorpe people know only too well, until fairly recent years, that stretch of land going from what used to be the Lysaghts Works down to the Trent and Flixborough was allowed to remain untouched. But today, all has changed there apart from one significant area, known as Ackie's Warren, after Sir Berkeley's gamekeeper Walter Atkinson, mentioned in chapter five. That area is still wooded and interesting for naturalists, but to the east there are massive factories and to the south there is a retail park, as is the modern way. Atkinson's home was down in the Warren and today merely the foundation indentations remain.

Sir Berkeley's influence on the Crosby area (now part of Scunthorpe) was wide and deep. In 2008, there was an insight into this when the *Scunthorpe Evening Telegraph* produced a feature on St George's Church in Crosby. In a flower festival programme from the 1920s, Ted Burks had written about the origins of the church, and Ted was quoted:

> It is impossible to mention any name in particular because Crosby is indebted to so many – both adults and children. However, mention must be made of our patrons, the Sheffield family, whose generosity and interest in Crosby has been invaluable over so many years.

It had been a long struggle: as the report notes, the first version of the church had been 'a corrugated iron building on Frodingham Road – known affectionately as the "tin tabernacle", or "tin tab"'.

In those post-war years there were other battles for Sir Berkeley to fight as well. In October 1920, the Hall had Excess Mineral Rights Duty imposed. It was just one of the many pressures on the landed aristocracy and the new landholders too, in a world that had radically changed after the gargantuan struggles of the war. Sir Berkeley appealed against these assessments, which concerned ironstone mined at Frodingham Moor. At that time, before the development of steel production on a large scale, there was extensive mining going on around the area. This was dangerous work for the labourers, who had to work by pushing large wheelbarrows of ore across diggings that were 30 feet deep.

Sir Berkeley's assessment had been £2,300 for one of the war years. In modern terms, that is well over £100,000. A whole team of administrators and assessors gave evidence on behalf of Sir Berkeley, but their argument that there were different qualities of ore in the area was countered by an academic expert dragged in by the Inland Revenue, who said, 'The Frodingham ores were lean ores; therefore nearly all the mines had steelworks connected with them, and the ores were used direct for steelmaking.' Sir Berkeley's camp were claiming that Frodingham and Cleveland ores were dissimilar. In fact, the Hall had received only £143 in excess income.

There was, of course, the estate village of Normanby as an important part of the scene. There was the Home Farm and the cottages, tied, for the workpeople of the estate. When the present Hall was built in about the late 1820s, some of the farm cottages were constructed at the same time. A century later, offices and workers' cottages were built, as the Hall and the family's enterprises expanded, and Sir Berkeley enriched both his cultural life and his family's status in the higher echelons of the nobility (hence his London property, and much more). The village itself is in a very attractive location on an escarpment leading away from the long geological incline known as the Lincolnshire Edge.

The first decades of the twentieth century saw the development of workers' housing estates on country house land, partly as a definite, visible move towards creating a semblance of a rural idyll. It coincided with such artistic and cultural movements as English folk song and folk dance, Arts and Crafts furniture and the new garden towns around London. Normanby was very much in step with this element in the *Zeitgeist*. Nikolaus Pevsner, in his detailed work on Lincolnshire architecture, explains this feature in rather more open and general terms; he refers to it as a 'speciality' of Lincolnshire and adds that they were 'an expression of philanthropy, good estate management, or just an unselfconscious growth'. Either way, they were, at Normanby, designed in the estate workshops.

At this juncture, mention must be made of Charles Winn, a man whose family made a deep imprint on the history of Scunthorpe and of Normanby. His family were from Nostell Priory, Wakefield, and as mentioned previously, he married Harriette Dumaresq. Winn looked for the ironstone on his land and when this was seen to be the future for him, he marketed his product. His son Rowland was to be MP for Pontefract from 1868. He was born in 1820, and lived until 1893.

Rowland Winn, later Lord St Oswald, also planned a 'garden village', which was to be alongside Rowland Road. This was conceived by the board of the Redbourn Hill Ironworks in 1919, and the new area was to be known as New Frodingham. James Foster, who has studied the project in depth, explained the limitations of the 'vision':

> Winn's terraced houses ... were only 14 feet wide and there was a 3-foot passageway through to the second room, thus the front room was approximately 10 feet 6 inches wide. ... There were no front gardens, but some houses boasted a grassed area at the rear, no more than 6 feet square. In some streets, the bath, a rare facility, was at the rear of a small annexed single storey kitchen, with the WC and coalhouse situated outside.

Ann Mitson and Barrie Cox, in an essay on the estate houses phenomenon, focus on the Yarborough estate, a short way across North Lincolnshire from Normanby. They emphasize the more artistic sources for the homes, saying that they were 'clearly designed to impress, to provide aesthetic pleasure for the owners and ... to create a picturesque image of idyllic contentment among the labouring population as much as to provide good, spacious, sanitary accommodation for employees.'

In 1919, the Normanby Estate Co was created as a private company, and *The Yorkshire Post* summarized:

The signatories to the memorandum of association ... are: Sir Berkeley Sheffield, and H.G. Atkinson-Clark, Estate Office, Crosby, Scunthorpe. Estate agent.... The permanent directors are: Sir Berkeley, Lord Arthur Hugh Grosvenor, Sir Samuel Scott, Lionel Faudel-Phillips and H.G. Atkinson-Clark.

There was his racing friend, Sir Samuel, and some family members. In a world of increasing financial complexity, Sir Berkeley was being conservative and cautious, having friends around him and keeping what he could 'in the family'.

The Great War years and the inter-war years brought all kinds of new stresses and strains on the landed aristocracy. The source of many of these political manoeuvres was in the so-called 'People's Budget' of 1909. Lloyd George was Chancellor of the Exchequer in 1908; he was a Liberal at a time when the new Labour Party was rising, and the mood in the air was to reform the House of Lords. Radical moves were blocked by the responses to bills being read in the Lords. But in 1909, Lloyd George proposed a new budget, which he described as an instrument in 'implacable warfare against poverty and squalidness'. He made an excessively long speech on his proposals, and that never wins much sympathy.

Some of the proposals were radical in the extreme, such as imposing a super tax on the very rich, and a capital gains tax, which would really lie heavily on those with solid unearned income such as landowners. There were severe arguments, debates and hotly discussed points of view, and naturally it was defeated in the Upper House. But he pressed on, and we can gain the tenor of his speeches on the theme with a look at what he said in Newcastle: 'A fully equipped duke costs as much to keep as two dreadnoughts [battleships] and they are just as great a terror – and they last longer.'

The vote was decidedly against the bill, on 30 November, but then there was an upheaval in Parliament when at a general election the Liberals had a majority of a mere two seats; there was a coalition and now the 'People's Budget' was passed. Richard Cavendish, writing in the journal *History Today*, commented on Lloyd George:

Brought up in poverty in Wales after his father's death when he was a baby, David Lloyd George grew up with a magnetic personality and a profound sympathy with the poor. He visited the House of Commons when he was 18 and confided to his diary that he viewed the assembly in the same spirit as William the Conqueror must have contemplated the England of Edward the Confessor.

He certainly caused a revolution with that budget.

There were confrontations between the very rich and the Inland Revenue on the various taxes, and newspapers saw this as a guarantee of grasping higher sales. One headline in 1919 read, 'Income tax inquiry: how super-tax is avoided'. As far as the Sheffields were concerned, the burdens of the People's Budget and the new taxation came along with the other effects of modernity and world war – everything from changes in working-class employment to new technology played a part. But the social context also had elements that had always been there, such as Sir Berkeley's horseracing and Shire horses; the need for a good education for the children; and of course, the shoots and the management of the now changing landscape around the Hall and Park.

There may have been troubles and even revolutions on the greater stage of world or national events, but around the villages of Burton, Normanby, Winterton and others, there was always the Hall to be relied on for cultural and recreational pursuits as well as for employment. The longstanding English traditions of local entertainment and 'doing a turn' were always popular, and professional entertainers were drafted in for those colourful events that filled the seasonal calendar. There may have been bonfires, children's parties, horse shows, flower shows and even athletics contests, but the favourite, up and down the land, was always the event that brought in some special attractions. Villages had their 'feasts' and fairs, but at the Hall, there were VIPs and music, speeches and surprise attractions.

There is no doubt that the Sheffields always relished an open-air entertainment, and who cared about the English weather? It was all about enjoying yourself. The list of the Hall's favourite spectacles and offerings includes bands, Shire horse shows, military displays and fireworks, and everything was done efficiently. There was, naturally, a committee involved in planning these events, and it is clear that Lady Sheffield and Sir Berkeley welcomed the occasional celebration of their locality and their community. Edith Spilman's point about the lady of the house scrubbing tables rings true. We have the sense that everyone pitched in.

Maud Mary Knott, quoted earlier in this chapter, recalled a typical fete, and her father was officiating too:

> In the early 1930s, the local Conservative party frequently held garden fetes at Normanby Hall.... Father was always responsible for the catering of drinks and crisps, so all the family went to help, and I remember sitting down at tea at a table in the courtyard with several of the titled relatives of the Sheffields who came down for the occasion.

The boat was well and truly pushed out in October 1933, when Scunthorpe received a royal visit – that of Prince George. The press announced the visit with an account of the planned itinerary: 'This includes a tour of the local steel works, a visit to the new trunk road and the opening of the new nurses' home.' Not very inspiring, one might think, except in terms of HRH looking impressed at industrial and practical advances. But of course, there were the Sheffields:

> Prince George will stay two nights in North Lincolnshire as the guest of Sir Berkeley Sheffield.... His programme for a full day in the town will also include the inspection of a rally of Lincolnshire ex-servicemen and there will probably be a civic ball in the evening.

When HRH Prince George did arrive, the *Hull Daily Mail* made a point of including the Hall, of course: 'Lunch was taken at Normanby Hall, where others present included Lord Yarborough, Lord Heneage, chairman of the Lindsey County Council ... and Councillor E. Kennedy of the Scunthorpe UDC.' Anyone today living in or driving through Scunthorpe, cannot fail to know that the arterial road through is split at a roundabout now with a Beefeater pub. The two halves are Kingsway and Queensway, and the names stem from that royal visit, when Prince George declared the road open and gave the names of the two sections.

The social history really means *social* – in the fullest sense. One way to see exactly what kind of activity took place that helps us to understand today what community entertainment involved then, is to look at brochures and booklets. In 1954, for instance, a 'Rally and Fete' was held at the Hall. The programme was this:

1.30 pm	GATES OPEN
2.00 pm	THE BARNETBY SILVER PRIZE BAND
2.30 pm	OPENING CEREMONY by the Rt. Hon. Sir WALTER WOMERSLEY, Bart. PC, JP
3.00 pm	TEAS will be served
4.30 pm	THE SUPREME AQUATIC SHOW
5.00 pm	LICENSED TENT OPENS
5.00 pm	CLAY PIGEON SHOOT commences
5.30 pm	RALLY MEETING
	Mr ROBERT TURTON, MC, JP, MP Parliamentary Secretary to Ministry of Pensions and National Insurance
7.00 pm	Second performance SUPREME AQUATIC SHOW
7.45 pm	VARIETY CONCERT

Of course, there would be a rolling programme of such things as Lucky Dip for Bottle or skittles as well, and a good competition was always welcome.

As the twentieth century progressed, and the mass media became more interested in the subject of celebrity, aristocrats attracted the journalists and scandal hunters. By the 1930s, any tit-bit of news concerning anyone famous or infamous attracted attention, and from time to time, the Sheffields were the subject of such scrutiny. This was the case in 1933, when a man from the *Hull Daily Mail* called at the Hall during a weekend shoot. The reason for this concerned the notoriety of a certain Glen Kidston, perhaps only known today to aficionados of motor sport and the inter-war years of hedonism and adventure.

Two years before the journalist called with his questions, in the Drakensburg Mountains on the borderland between Natal and Basutoland, Lieutenant Commander Glen Kidston was flying with a friend, Captain Gladstone. They both died; a witness, as the press reported, saw 'the plane flying over the peaks in a terrible storm, when it suddenly turned turtle and crashed'. There was a rumour, in 1933, that Kidston's widow, Nancy, neé Soames, was now engaged to Edmund, Sir Berkeley's son. Of course, it turned out to be true and they did marry, but the newspaper report gives the modern reader a clear insight into the fledgling world of magazine gossip and celebrity culture:

> On good authority it was ascertained that the announcement of Mr Reginald Sheffield's engagement was extremely premature. It was without doubt true that he had been seen in Mrs Kidston's company recently, but no definite announcement was expected for some considerable time.

The current Sir Reginald is the son of Edmund and Nancy, and the father of Samantha Cameron.

As for Glen Kidston, he was certainly a star celebrity, being known as one of the 'Bentley Boys' – a set of society swells and playboys. In the Great War he was a naval officer and he survived two torpedo attacks on ships he served on. He then served on board HMS *Orion* and was in action at the famous Battle of Jutland. He became an enthusiast for submarines and had a near-death experience during trials for the X1 sub. After the war, the passion for land speed came along and he was involved in any event entailing high speed, including the TT races on the Isle of Man. Just a few years before the fatal crash in South Africa, he had survived another crash, in which he was a true hero, trying to save the life of Prince Eugen von Schaumberg-Lippe; he went back into the wreck of their plane, which was flying to Amsterdam from Croyden, and brought out the Prince, who unfortunately did not survive. His impact on women as well as on the media was profound; it seems that at his death, his lovers' names came out, and these included Barbara Cartland, Pola Negri and Margaret Whigham (later the Duchess of Argyll).

There was also sport, which was always part of the scene, and in particular, there was cricket. This was such an important pursuit for the gentry that the arranged matches took on a supreme importance in the year's social calendar. Down in Sussex, for instance, the Earl of Sheffield (nothing to do with the Normanby or Musgrave families) actually had a railway station built by his Sheffield Park ground, and that became the location for the first matches against Australia.

At Normanby, the Normanby Park Cricket Club was the star attraction in this respect, being established in 1900. As David Taylor pointed out in his book on Normanby,:

> Matches were friendly fixtures of one innings duration with no over limits, captains declaring when they thought fit. The players either lived in Normanby village or were local farmers or professional people. ...
> Hockey was played in the winter months, but not football.

There was also a 'Cricket Week' every year, which entailed invitation games, in the solid English tradition of the teams being labelled by the sponsor, becoming such outfits as 'Lady Sheffield's XI' or similar. It was all taken very seriously in spite of the good humour, and the sport was there for all ages, because in 1926 a junior team was created, being the brainchild of a local solicitor called George Davy. These became the Normanby Park Colts.

The Normanby village teachers also made their mark. David Taylor, in his book on the Hall, points out that the teacher always lived in the same house; until 1930, the teacher was a character called Mr Wilkes, who had the nickname of 'Gaffer', and his school covered the cluster of villages around the Hall. He had a rent-free house, and this was on the village street, close to the Hall. There were two assistant teachers, and of course, in those days, teachers had real authority. One memory of him touches on this:

> The boys who lived in Normanby could go home at playtime and we used to go into the field on Scunthorpe Road and play cricket or football. Then when our time was up, old Gaffer Wilkes would walk out ... and blow a whistle, then we would wander round and back to school.

More recently, in the last phase of the Hall's story up to its being taken into the responsibility of the local Borough Council, the teacher was Thomas Sumpter, a name well known to most Scunthorpe residents as, until recently with the arrival of academies, a comprehensive school was named after him. He was the last teacher in the village, and memories of him are complimentary; he was indeed a remarkable man. He was later to become Head of Brumby Secondary School as well as at Westcliff, which later became the Thomas Sumpter School. One memory of him notes that he was 'a very keen sportsman, very keen on his cricket and hockey.... He was also very keen on the Scunthorpe Music and Drama Festival, and his pupils regularly won prizes for singing and elocution.'

Today, there are very few survivors of the celebrated social and cultural features of the Hall as it was in its last decades. But one that does survive is Joey. He was the Park's most famous deer, and in 2008, the *Scunthorpe Evening Telegraph* ran a feature on him, noting:

> For six years, he was fearlessly at the head of twenty-five red deer and forty-five fallow deer ... and reigned supreme until his death in 1979. According to reports ... at the time, this happened during the rutting season, and because of his age – he was thought to be 15 – he became exhausted while fighting.

Today, thanks to the art of taxidermy, Joey sits in the small information booth at the Hall. Apparently, he used to walk up behind anglers and stick his nose into their food supplies, and he was even featured on a Christmas card. Somehow, Joey seems to symbolize that world that has been erased by time.

Conclusions

Sir Roger told them, with the air of a man who would not give his judgement rashly, that much might be said on both sides.

The Spectator 28, Joseph Addison

Conclusions to books invite sweeping statements and summaries of judgements; but it has to be said that looking deeply into this microcosm of a country estate from the great days of rural England has not led me to such grand opinions, nor to any new species of wisdom. What I would like to emphasize is the sheer efficiency of the Hall and everyone who kept it going over the centuries. It was at once a massive business concern and a family home; it was both a symbol of past values and a celebration of contemporary life. Yet underpinning all these features has been the acceptance by all the Sheffields who have run the place that it has been of the utmost importance to preserve as much of the status quo as possible, under the threats of modernity and accelerating social change. That has to command respect.

At the same time, there have been no rosy-coloured spectacles through which to view this lost world; I have looked steadily and long at the ways in which time was filled and objectives were met, and it is remarkable just how much success the urge to conserve and preserve has been evident. Although today the Hall and its environs are cared for by Scunthorpe Borough Council, and although official guides meet the visitor, instead of family members, essentially, a visit there provides a clear and compelling impression of what has always been on offer: the grandeur, the vistas, and the spirit of aristocratic serenity it exudes.

Sometimes in social history, one finds that the everyday material culture of a person or a place tells the reader a great deal. This is the case with Normanby Hall. The first scrap of paper to catch my attention when rifling through a box of ephemera from the estate's history was a pro forma letterhead with 'Normanby Estates: Agricultural and horticultural society' at the top and the details of telegrams, telephone, and the names 'President: Sir Berkeley Sheffield' and 'Hon. Secretary: W.S. Medlicott'.

This little letterhead says so much about the Hall in the mid-twentieth century. It conveys a place of business, but it has the name of an aristocrat on it; the communication details pre-date our modern world of landlines, mobiles and faxes, but the insistence on a suggested efficiency is there in the print. It had been produced by a local printer and then delivered in cardboard boxes.

This scrap of paper pushed me to ask more questions and to make that effort of imagination that writers and historians need when trying to evoke and bring to life a long-gone culture. When Leonard Woolf, husband of Virginia, came back from six years in Ceylon in 1911, he sensed that he had missed a radical, fundamental change in his home country. He wrote that the people in the countryside seemed closer to the England of Chaucer than they did to 1963 (when he was writing his autobiography). There was something of that sense in me as I went a little deeper into Normanby history. What struck me repeatedly was the truth of what the Russian novelist, Ivan Turgenev, wrote in his novel of 1862, *Fathers and Sons*, which deals partly with the problems of a country estate in times of social upheaval: 'Remember my dear sir,' he repeated acidly, 'the aristocrats of England. They do not give up one iota of their rights, and that is why they respect the rights of others; they demand what is due to them, and that is why they themselves perform what is due to them.'

The research for this has made me look again at the country house. Over the years I have joined the throng in the usual guided tour of some noble old pile with its huge rooms, Greek columns and array of portraits in oils; I have looked in astonishment at the relics and display of items brought home by aristocrats after their European Grand Tours; I have even looked in awe at such material wealth as a fine library with thousands of leather-bound volumes on the shelves. But looking at Normanby Hall with an intention to find and root out its stories has changed my attitudes and opinions of the English country estate.

I now see that there have been extreme and tenacious struggles for survival as well as the enjoyment of immense wealth and privilege. I understand the stresses and strains of maintaining so much land, so much house and so many dependent people. Of all the documents I have pored over, the one that stands out is not a legal document in parchment or a proclamation of political vies; no, it is a statement of accounts from 1931, with such items as 'Expenses – temporary nurse' and 'Insurances' on it. This is all so normal, so *human*. One has to say that, after all, for all the pomp and circumstance and all the letters after people's names, this has been a family story.

Looking at the Hall from top to bottom in the social hierarchy also brings rewards of special insight. Most modern readers are accustomed to seeing the working lives of servants depicted, thanks to a genre of memoirs started perhaps by Margaret Powell in 1968 with her book *Below Stairs*, and continued into *Downton Abbey* and *Upstairs, Downstairs*, but there is still a strange and compelling interest in those submerged lives of dedicated hard graft, and one of my principle conclusions is a feeling of awe and respect for those workers.

The historian who turns attention to such a strictly class-created institution as a country estate might easily find a number of criticisms because revisionary interpretations of land and power by one branch of writers has found exploitation and suppression, but one of the many pleasant surprises found is the realization that workers enjoyed their days at the Hall and Park, on the whole. The pleasures and recreations seem to have counterbalanced the hard work very well, and of course, in about 1850 and again in about 1950, expectations and career aspirations were certainly not what they are today. In fact, such is the bond between estate and workers that when a house fails and fades away, the results are not really appreciated by town dwellers. In their biography of Gervase Elwes, Wilfrida and Roland Elwes make this point:

> Whenever a landowner dies, land is thrown upon the market with the result that what was a tradition becomes merely a security for investment.... The seller, whose family has usually loved it for generations, is replaced by a buyer whose only concern is to make his profit and get out.

Fortunately, this did not happen at Normanby.

Of course, there are aspects of the country house life that are always open to criticism; the lives of the farm workers were undoubtedly hard, and the tied cottages did not help. As one labourer put it, 'The majority of village people worked in the village ... you either lived in an estate cottage or a farm cottage, and if you lost your job you lost your house.' It wasn't until the Agricultural Holdings Act of 1948 that this changed.

On the whole, then, I feel that my social history has revealed some happy surprises and brought back into the light some dramatic tales from a very different world. As L.P. Hartley famously said, in *The Go-Between*, 'The past is a foreign country: they do things differently there.' Broadly speaking, that world of Normanby, now long gone and in the annals of North Lincolnshire history, was a happy place to be.

As most historians must surely feel, the investigations into past times that have been so necessary in producing the book, have revealed surprises; if I had to pick out just one of these, it would be the myths of decline and ruin with reference to the inter-war years, and Adrian Tinniswood, author of *The Long Weekend: Life in the English Country Houses Between the Wars* (2016), points out, 'What surprised me was the parallel story that emerged of a vibrant social world in which the country house managed not only to survive, but to prosper.' Part of that success is vividly illustrated at Normanby Hall – the tendency for many of the estate owners to move closer to their workers and their house servants. Sir Berkeley and Lady Sheffield, as the vernacular phrase has it, 'mucked in' when required, and knew their domain from top to bottom.

Today, while one might expect a certain level of blandness as the Park and Hall are in the hands of an organization rather than a family, the good news is that it is not a difficult task to enter that world now lost, with a little imagination, that is. After all, sitting outside the little café in the stable yard, there is nothing changed or added to the actual stable and to the buildings now housing old vehicles from what it was in the Regency years. The peacocks still make their screeching appeal and there is a leisurely air around the place, evoking a little of what it must have been like when work went on and horses stamped and neighed, carriages were cleaned and brickwork scrubbed.

Entering the Hall itself, little has changed from what was there in about 1920, in spite of the replacement furnishings; imagining the baronets at their desk or surveying the deer park after breakfast is easily indulged. The vista is as pleasing as it would have been to the first Sir Robert as his mind worked overtime, conceiving savings and planning increased yields. In fact, still today, with a little thought, the easy mix of workplace and family home is very much present. Looking into that mixture in the historical chronicle has revealed unexpected phases of life, new impressions of people, and most of all, so many interesting stories in the offshoots into the history in the family footnotes that one is tempted to misquote Samuel Johnson's phrase about London: 'When a man is tired of Normanby, he is tired of life.' The historian finds that such a comment applies because Normanby, as was the case with all the best, most ambitious country houses and estates, made every effort to be a presence in the local area. Yes, one could easily pick out the profit motive and political ambition as the central driving forces behind their lives, but when was that ever a terrible sin? Those imperatives tend to create, establish and build lasting legacies of wealth and enterprise.

The detachment of the social historian is always essential; my leanings are towards Marxism, and so it would be a simple but very reductive task to interpret aristocratic lives with a Marxist critique, but that in itself generates such a distorted picture that the search for truth is blurred.

Acknowledgements

Many people have helped with the research for this book. Thanks are due to staff at Scunthorpe Museum and at the archives office in Grimsby Town Hall, in particular, Evelyn van Breemen and Madeleine Grout at the North Lincolnshire Museum; William Pocklington and David Jones at *Fieldsports* magazine; Katie Thompson at the Tank Museum; and Jennie Cartwright and Phil Melladay at the archives in Grimsby Town Hall. I must also thank these individuals for their help as they kindly responded to my appeals for help: Nick Doust, Steve Race, and Bryan Longbone. Bryan was extremely helpful with the more financial and economics areas in the sources, and the results were markedly interesting. His work on the North Lindsey Light Railway was invaluable too.

There was also plenty of assistance from Caroline Bingham, editor of *Lincolnshire Life,* and Justin, of *Country Life* magazine, and from those involved in the heritage work for Burton-upon-Stather, notably Valerie Mercer, who provided biographical details about her father. Clare Hardwick, at *County Life,* helped with the access to the Matthew Grass material.

At Scunthorpe Central Library, Tim Davies was very helpful in smoothing the path towards finding additional sources for some of the historical footnotes.

For information on the Dumaresq family of the Channel Islands, thanks go to John Jackson.

Thanks also to John Robinson for his estate work memoirs.

Bibliography and Sources

BOOKS

Note: dates of first publication are in brackets before the citation of the edition used.

Works cited

Armstrong, M. Elizabeth (Ed.), *An Industrial Island: A History of Scunthorpe*, Scunthorpe Borough Museum & Art Gallery, 1981.

Askwith, Richard, *The Lost Village: in search of a forgotten rural England*, Ebury Press, 2008.

Austen, Jane, *Mansfield Park* (1814), Penguin, 1996.

Bailey, Chris, & Bramley, Steve, *The 1/5th Battalion Lincolnshire Regiment in the Great War*, Iron Mariner, 2015.

Beastall, T.W., *Agricultural Revolution in Lincolnshire*, The History of Lincs Committee, 1978.

Bennett, Stewart & Bennett, Nicholas, *An Historical Atlas of Lincolnshire*, The University of Hull Press, 1993.

Blythe, Ronald, *Akenfield* (1969), Penguin, 1975.

Bott, Alan, *Our Fathers*, Heinemann, 1901.

Campion, G. Edward, *Lincolnshire Dialects*, Richard Kay, 2013.

Chivers, Keith, *The Shire Horse*, Futura Publications, 1996.

Cook, Chris, *Britain in the Nineteenth Century, 1815–1914*, Routledge, 2005.

Cooke, Reg & Cooke, Peter, *Scunthorpe's Industries*, Tempus, 1999.

Crook, J. Mordaunt, *The Rise of the Nouveaux Riches*, John Murray, 1999.

Elwes, Wilfrida & Roland, *Gervase Elwes*, Grayson & Grayson, 1935.

Ffrench, Yvonne (compiler), *News from the Past 1805–1887*, Gollancz, 1888.

Fisher, H.A., *The History of Kirton Lindsey*, Spiegl Press, 1981.

George, David Lloyd, *War Memoirs Volume 3*, Ivor Nicholson & Watson, 1933.

Gray, Adrian, *Crime and Criminals in Victorian Lincolnshire*, Paul Watkins, 1993.

Haggard, H. Rider, *A Farmer's Year*, Cresset Library, 1987.

Hamilton, John, *The Manuscript in a Red Box* (1904), Isle of Axholme Family History Society, 1999.

Hawkins, Rev. W.M., *Key to the Tithe Question*, Hamilton, Adams, 1887.

Johnson, Dr Samuel, *Lives of the Poets (1779–1781)*, Oxford University Press, 1973.

Jones, David S.D., *Mr Grass the Gamekeeper*, the author, 1984.

Jarvis, Francis Amcotts, *The Parish of Burton-upon-Stather with Flixborough*, S. Forsaith, 1922.

Kelly's Directories Ltd., *Kelly's Directory of Lincolnshire*, Kelly's, 1933.

Langlands, Alex, Ginn, Peter & Goodman, Ruth, *Victorian Farm*, Pavilion, 2008.

Lethbridge, Lucy, *Servants: a Downstairs View of Twentieth-century Britain*, Bloomsbury, 2013.

McCarthy, Patricia, *Life in the Country House in Georgian Ireland*, Yale University Press, 2016.

Parr, Martin, *Calderdale Photographs*, Calderdale Museum Service, 1984.

Pevsner, Nicholas & Harris, John, *The Buildings of England: Lincolnshire*, Penguin, 1964.

Pye, Michael, *The Edge of the World*, Penguin, 2015.

Rawnsley, W.F., *Highways and Byways in Lincolnshire*, Macmillan, 1926.

Readhead, Winn, *Stather Tales: reminiscences of a wartime childhood in the Lincolnshire village of Burton-upon-Stather*, the author, 2004.

Ridley, Jane, *Bertie: a Life of Edward VI*, Vintage, 2013.

Rose, Rev. H.J., *A New General Biographical Dictionary*, Fellowes, 1818.

Scotland, Lt Col A.P., *The London Cage*, Evans Brothers, 1957, expurgated.

Sherburn, George, *The Early Career of Alexander Pope*, Oxford University Press, 1934.

Skehel, Mona, *Tales from the Showyard: two hundred years of agricultural shows in Lincolnshire*, Lincolnshire Agricultural Society, 1999.

Stobart, Mrs St Clair, *War and Women*, G. Bell & sons, 1913.

Swingler, Molly E.D., *Scunthorpe's Second Freeman: the story of Harold E. Dudley*, the author, 1995.

Taylor, David J., *I Remember Normandy: Life on a Lincolnshire Estate Between the Wars*, Hutton Press Ltd., 1994.

Tinniswood, Adrian, *The Long Weekend: Life in the English Country House 1918–1939*, Jonathan Cape, 2016.

Turgeney, Ivan, *Fathers and Sons* (1862), Penguin, 2009.

Vincent, John (Ed.), *The Crawford Papers: The Journals of David Lindsay, Twenty-Seventh Earl of Crawford*, Manchester University Press, 1984.

White, William, *History, Gazetteer and Directory of Lincolnshire* (1856), David & Charles Reprints, 1977.

White, William, *History, Gazetteer and Directory of the City and Diocese of Lincoln*, William White, 1882.

Wilde, Oscar, *An Ideal Husband* (1895) in *The Importance of Being Earnest and Other Plays*, Vintage, 2016.

Wilde, Oscar, *The Importance of Being Earnest* (1895), in Holland, Vyvyan, (Ed.), *Complete Works of Oscar Wilde*, Collins, 1969.

Wrench, John Evelyn, *Alfred Lord Milner: the man of no illusions*, Eyre & Spottiswoode, 1958.

Reference works consulted and for further reading

Broadbent, Susie *et alia*, *The Crosby Angel: a community's war memorial*, Friends of the Crosby Angel, Scunthorpe, 2008.

Cannon, John, *Oxford Dictionary of British History*, OUP, 2001.

Cook, Chris, *Britain in the Nineteenth Century 1815–1914*, Routledge, 2005.

Cowie, L.W., *The Wordsworth Dictionary of British Social History* (1973), Wordsworth, 1996.

Dolby, I.E.A. (Ed.), *The Journal of the Royal Horse Guards for the year 1871*, Clowes, 1871.

Drabble, Margaret, *The Oxford Companion to English Literature*, Oxford University Press, 1987.

Mee, Arthur, *The King's England: Lincolnshire*, Hodder & Stoughton, 1949.

Richardson, John, *The Local Historian's Encyclopaedia*, Historical Publications, 1974.

Ward-Jackson, C.H. & Harvey, Denis E., *The English Gypsy Caravan*, David & Charles, 1972.

Articles in newspapers and periodicals

Anon, 'Fiction: Napoleon Boswell', *The Spectator*, 31 May 1913, p.28.

Cavendish, Richard, 'The House of Lords Rejects the People's Budget', *History Today* vol.59, issue 11 November 2009, pp.9–10.

Chronicle: *Annual Register* for 1844, p.31.

Dudley, Edith Spilman, 'Lady Sheffield, Gracious, Gifted and Well-Beloved', in *Scunthorpe Star*, 15 July 1952, p.3.

Duguid, Lindsay, 'Homes and Gardens', *Times Literary Supplement*, 1 July 2016, pp.12–13.

Foster, James, 'The Redbourn Garden Village Trust', *Lincolnshire Past and Present* No. 94, Winter 2013–14, pp.11–15.

'Ironstone Area Amalgamation', *Hull Times*, 5 October 1918, p.4.

Jones, David, 'A Lincolnshire Gamekeeper', in *The Lincolnshire Poacher* (*County Life*, 2001), pp.55–58.

Knott, Maud Mary, 'Scunthorpe Memories', *Lincolnshire Life*, November 1987, pp.29–31.

Lewis, Roger, 'Sorry I Shot Your Dog Old Boy', *Daily Mail*, 27 May 2016, pp.60–61.

Longbone, Bryan, 'The North Lindsey Light Railway', *Forward: journal of the GCR Society* No. 149, September 2006, pp.27–31 (see www.gcrsociety.co.uk/ Forward_149_web.pdf).

'L.W.' (name unknown), 'Normanby Park, The Seat of Sir Berkeley Sheffield', *Country Life*, 20 July 1911, pp.170–176.

Mitson, Anne, & Cox, Barrie, 'Victorian Estate Housing on the Yarborough Estate', in *Rural History* vol. 6, issue 1, April 1995, pp.29–45.

'Normanby Estate', in *The Yorkshire Post*, 26 September 1919, p.24.

Parker, Charles, 'T. & J. Fletcher of Winterton', in *Ploughs, Chaff Cutters and Steam Engines*, Society for Lincolnshire History and Archaeology, 2007, pp.66–71.

Rothery, Janet, 'The General Election of 1945 in our part of North Lincolnshire', *The Lincolnshire Poacher*, Spring 2015, pp.17–26.

Scunthorpe Evening Telegraph features:

'Deer in a thousand lives on in people's affections', 24 December 2008, p.16.

'Worshippers taking trip down memory lane', 17 December 2005, p.16.

'Survey of London', in *Survey of London: The Grosvenor Estate in Mayfair, Part 2: The Buildings, vol. 40*, Legacy System, 1980.

Tinniswood, Adrian, 'The Long Weekend': interview in *The Daily Telegraph*, 25 June 2016, p.27.

Internet sources

www.brookvillageshistory.co.uk, 'Agricultural Wages and Tied Cottages'.

https://countryhousereader.wordpress.com.

genuki.cs.ncl.uk/DEV/DevonMisc/Insolvents 1769 html, written by Lindsey Withers.

Hansard Parliamentary reports for 1907, taken from the site https://hansard.parliament.uk/.

Jones, David S.D., 'A Gamekeeping Family in the Great War', www.fieldsports magazine.com.

'Juvenile Woman Suffragists', 'Edalji Case', 'Athenry Outrages' and 'Crime in Lincolnshire'.

Old Bailey records: www.oldbaileyonline.org/.

Port, M.H. & Thorne, R.G, Newbolt, John Henry, at www.historyofparliamentonline.org, 'Members 1790–1820'.

www.rmg.co.uk. The portrait of Edmund Sheffield is here, and notes are available on site.

Sheffield, Sir Reginald, *The History of the Sheffield Family*, on the Sutton Park, York, website: www.statelyhome.co.uk.

www.ssme.bakerbase.com/the_story.htm (website of the Scunthorpe Society of Model Engineers).

Westminster Abbey: see www.westminster-abbey.org, 'John Sheffield, Duke of Normanby and Family'.

Archives

Museum of English Rural Life: the Chivers Collection at Ref: D CHIV (see https:www.reading.ac.uk/merl/).

North Lincolnshire Archives: material relating to Sir Robert Sheffield; accounts and advice books 524 C/2/1-2; cuttings D/2/1; letters C/1/4 and 5; magistrate's notebook and records D/Z/8.

Ephemera

Clay, Charles, 'Welcome Home to Normanby!', printed sheet, the author at Messingham, 1876.

References were also made to the boxed ephemera collection held at the North Lincolnshire Museum, but no specific material was used: merely general comment.

Index